CW01617652

An Introduction to Mac OS X Mountain Lion

Andrew Edney

Bernard Babani (publishing) Ltd
The Grampians
Shepherds Bush Road
London W6 7NF
England
www.babanibooks.com

Please Note

Although every care has been taken with the production of this book to ensure that all information is correct at the time of writing and that any projects, designs, modifications and/or programs, etc. contained herewith, operate in a correct and safe manner and also that any components specified are normally available in Great Britain, the Publishers and Author(s) do not accept responsibility in any way for the failure (including fault in design) of any project, design, modification or program to work correctly or to cause damage to any equipment that it may be connected to or used in conjunction with, or in respect of any other damage or injury that may be so caused, nor do the Publishers accept responsibility in any way for the failure to obtain specified components.

Notice is also given that if equipment that is still under warranty is modified in any way or used or connected with home-built equipment then that warranty may be void.

ISBN 978 0 85934 736 5

First Published – September 2012

British Library Cataloguing in Publication Data:

A catalogue record for this book is available from the British Library.

Printed and bound in Great Britain for Bernard Babani (publishing) Ltd

About this Book

With Apple MacBooks becoming more popular, and there being a choice of different models (the MacBook, the MacBook Pro and the MacBook Air), more people are trying Macs for the first time.

If you have spent years using a Microsoft Windows computer then using a Mac for the first time can be a little confusing at times.

This is where this book comes in. We will provide a gentle introduction into the world of the Apple Mac, so giving you enough knowledge and confidence to get out there and do so much more with your Mac than you realised.

What you will learn about in this book isn't just confined to the laptops – you can use most, if not all of the knowledge on any Apple Mac system, including the Mac Mini and the iMac – basically any Apple device running OS X Mountain Lion.

This book is an independent publication and has not been endorsed by Apple Inc.

Acknowledgements

I would like to offer my thanks to my family and friends for their support and assistance during the long months of writing this book.

I would also like to offer my thanks to all the staff at Babani for once again publishing my book.

Primarily, thanks must go to Katy for her support and thanks to Apollo and Starbuck for keeping me calm when I got too stressed out.

To anyone I might have missed, a heartfelt thanks goes out to all of you for making this possible. It's been a pleasure.

About the Author

ANDREW EDNEY has been an IT professional for more than 15 years and has over the course of his career worked for a range of high-tech companies, such as Microsoft, Hewlett-Packard and Fujitsu Services. He has a wide range of experience in virtually all aspects of Microsoft's computing solutions, having designed and architected large enterprise solutions for government and private-sector customers. Over the years, Andrew has made a number of guest appearances at major industry events, presenting on a wide range of information systems subjects, such as an appearance at the annual Microsoft Exchange Conference in Nice where he addressed the Microsoft technical community on mobility computing. Andrew is currently involved in numerous Microsoft beta programs, including next-generation Windows operating systems and next-generation Microsoft Office products, and he actively participates in all Windows Media Center beta programs and was, and still is heavily involved in the Windows Home Server beta program.

Andrew is a Microsoft MVP for Windows Home Server.

Andrew also has a number of qualifications, including an MSc in Network Technologies and Management, he is an MCSE and has numerous MCPs. He is also a Certified Information Systems Security Professional (CISSP) and a Certified Ethical Hacker.

In addition, Andrew has written a number of books on topics such as Windows Home Server, Windows Media Center, Live Communications Server, PowerPoint 2007, networks, Windows Vista, and the Xbox 360. These include *The Windows Home Server User's Guide* (Apress, 2007), *Pro LCS: Live Communications Server Administration* (Apress, 2007), *Getting More from Your Microsoft Xbox 360* (Bernard Babani, 2006), *How to Set Up Your Home or Small Business Network* (Bernard Babani, 2006), *Using Microsoft Windows XP Media Center 2005* (Bernard Babani, 2006), *Windows Vista: An Ultimate Guide* (Bernard Babani, 2007), *PowerPoint 2007 in Easy Steps* (Computer Step, 2007), *Windows Vista Media Center in Easy Steps* (Computer Step, 2007), *Using Ubuntu Linux* (Bernard Babani, 2007), *PowerPoint 2010 in Easy Steps* (In Easy Steps, 2010), *Netbooks in Easy Steps* (In Easy Steps, 2010),*Windows 7 Tweaks Tips and Tricks* (Bernard Babani, 2010), *An Introduction to the MacBook* (Bernard Babani, 2011), *Working With Windows Small Business Server 2011 Essentials* (MS Press, 2011), *An Introduction to the iPad 2* (Bernard Babani, 2011) and *An Introduction to the New iPad* (Bernard Babani, 2012).

Andrew also runs his own IT consulting company, Firebird Consulting, and has a website dedicated to all things tech, which can be found at http://connecteddigitalworld.com.

CONNECTED
— DIGITAL WORLD —

Andrew lives in Surrey with his partner, Katy, and their two cats and is the proud owner of a MacBook Air.

Contents

Conventions

Throughout this book, you will see a number of information boxes, bounded with either a red line like this…

DESIGNATING A WARNING

…or indeed, a blue line, like this…

DESIGNATING A NOTE, POINT OF INTEREST OR USEFUL TIP

Procedures and walkthroughs are shown as numerical lists, like this:

1. Step 1
2. Step 2

Right-clicking on a Mac:

Whenever we mention right-clicking something, if you are not using a mouse then you can either press the Control key and then click on the track pad or press on the track pad with two fingers instead of one (see page (xiii)). Don't worry, you will get used to it!

URL's are shown as follows: http://connecteddigitalworld.com.

List of Keyboard Shortcuts

Did you know that you can perform a lot of functions on the Mac from the keyboard? Here is a list of some of the more useful keyboard shortcuts.

There are some special keys shown on the keyboard (as you can see below). So anywhere you are told to press either Shift, Command or Option, you know which key to press!

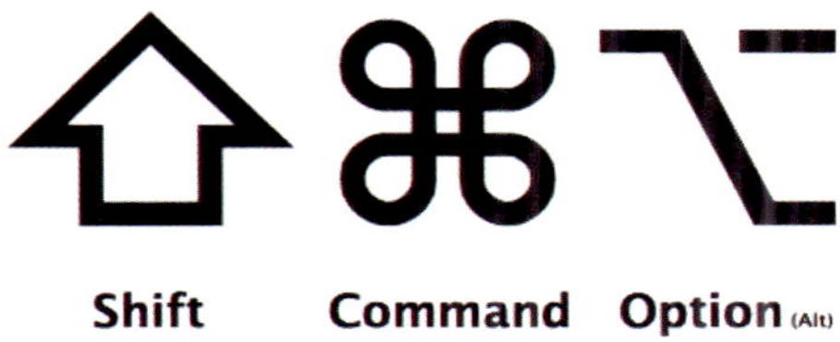

> Any of the keys shown below will need to be pressed together in order to use the shortcut – for example, if you want to copy something, you have to press the Command key and the C key together.

CUT : Command X

COPY : Command C

PASTE : Command V

SELECT ALL : Command A

UNDO : Command Z

REDO : Shift Command Z

NEW FINDER WINDOW : Command N

OPEN : Command O

GET INFO : Command I

VIEW AS ICONS : Command 1

VIEW AS LIST : Command 2

VIEW AS COLUMNS : Command 3

SHOW / HIDE TOOLBAR : Option Command T

SHOW VIEW OPTIONS : Command J

QUIT PROGRAM : Command Q

CLOSE WINDOW : Command W

Using the Multi-Touch Trackpad

There are a number of different things you can do with the multi-touch trackpad. Below are just a few to get you started.

Click – just use one finger to click.

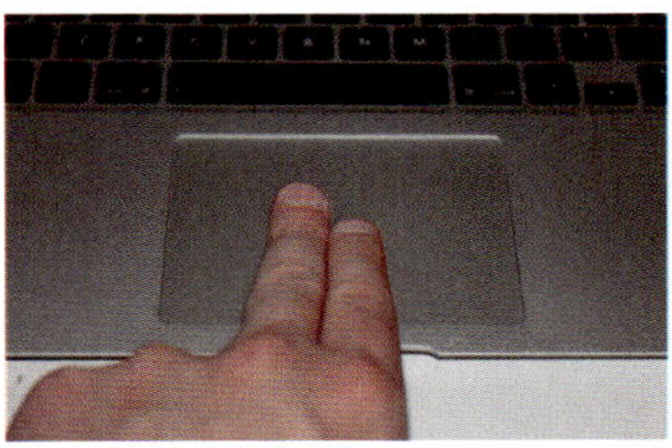

Right-click – if you press two fingers on the trackpad it is the equivalent of right-click on a mouse.

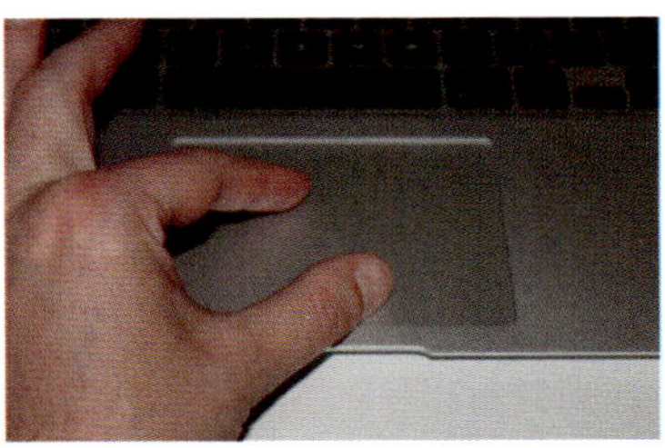

Pinch Open & Close – pinch to zoom in and out on photos, websites and more.

Ports on the MacBooks

Each MacBook has a different set of ports on them, and each revision may have something different. For example, the 2011 MacBook Pro's and Air's have a new Thunderbolt port which the earlier ones didn't. To give you an idea of what ports are included with the mid 2011 MacBook Air, have a look below.

The MacBook Air (mid 2011 version)

From left to right:

MagSafe – this is the power connector

USB 2.0 port – used for connecting USB devices

Headphones – used for connecting headphones

Microphone – used for connecting microphones

From left to right:

SD card slot – used for viewing photographs and other data from an SD card

USB 2.0 port – used for connecting USB devices

Thunderbolt port – used for connecting the MacBook Air to any Thunderbolt devices

The MacBook Air keyboard and trackpad:

Useful Websites

There are a number of very useful websites on the Internet that can help you with problems with your Mac, advice on hardware, guides and hints, and much more.

Some of the more useful ones are:

http://connecteddigitalworld.com/

http://www.maclife.com/

https://discussions.apple.com

http://www.macworld.com/

http://macfixit.com

http://www.apple.com

Why not add some of your own above?

1

Mac OS X 10.8 "Mountain Lion"

Just like Microsoft Windows, there have been many different versions of the Mac OS. The latest and greatest is OS X 10.8, also known as Mountain Lion.

When you buy a new Apple Mac (whether it is a MacBook, MacBook Pro or even the MacBook Air) your Mac will come pre-installed with Mountain Lion. Mountain Lion is designed to take advantage of the latest 64-bit hardware and comes with a whole host of very useful applications and features pre-installed ready for you to use.

Throughout this book we will be giving you an introduction to Mountain Lion and how to get your Mac up and running as quickly and as painlessly as possible.

Buying Mountain Lion

If you have an older Mac, then you may not have Mountain Lion installed. It is a good idea to always run the latest version of the software, and as this entire book is based on Mountain Lion you should upgrade now before continuing.

Fortunately the upgrade to Mountain Lion is very inexpensive. At the time of writing this book, you could buy it from the Apple App Store, as shown in Figure 1-1, for £13.99. To upgrade just follow the instructions after you have downloaded Mountain Lion.

Figure 1-1 Buying the Mountain Lion upgrade

> Before upgrading to Mountain Lion, make sure that you have all the latest updates installed.

Summary

Now that you know what Mountain Lion is, and you have your brand new Mac or an upgraded one sitting in front of you ready to go, it's time to switch it on and get started.

2

Switching On Your Mac for the First Time

The very first time you switch on your new Mac you will have to perform the initial set-up. This set-up includes choosing a language and time zone, creating an account and choosing a user account picture, and more.

The whole process of performing the initial set-up only takes a few minutes, but you should take your time and make sure that you select all the correct options for you.

So, to perform the initial set-up:

> Ensure your Mac is connected to a power source. The whole process only takes a few minutes to complete, but it is better to be safe than sorry!

1. Press the Power Button to start up the Mac and launch the Setup Assistant.
2. From the Welcome screen, select the Country or Region you are in from the list, as shown in Figure 2-1, and then click Continue.

Figure 2-1 The Welcome Screen

3. Select your keyboard layout, as shown in Figure 2-2, and click Continue.

> If for some reason your Country or Region isn't displayed, click on the Show All box to display every supported option.

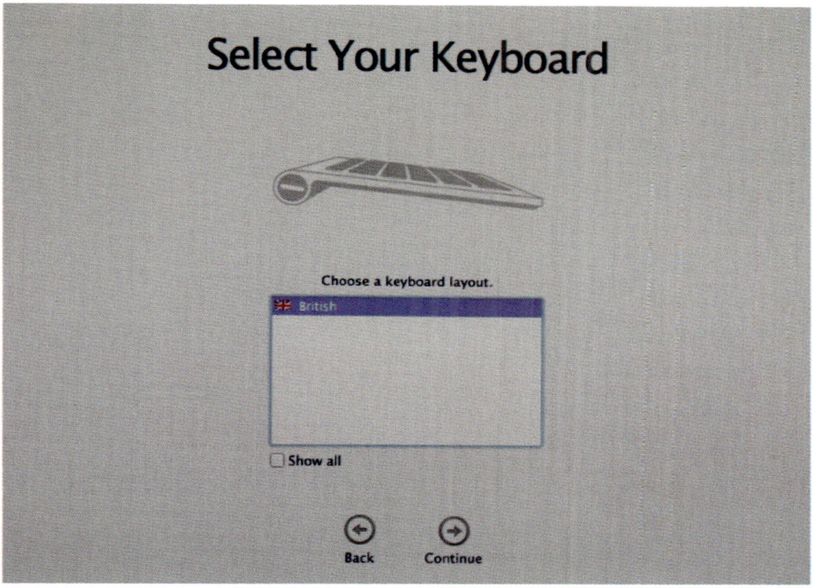

Figure 2-2 Selecting your keyboard layout

4. Now you can choose to join a Wireless Network by clicking on the Network name if it is shown and typing in the Network Password, as shown in Figure 2-3.

> If you do want to connect to a wireless network now, you need to make sure that the wireless network is operational and that you know both the wireless network name and also the password. If you don't know these you should find them out now, or wait until a later time to connect.

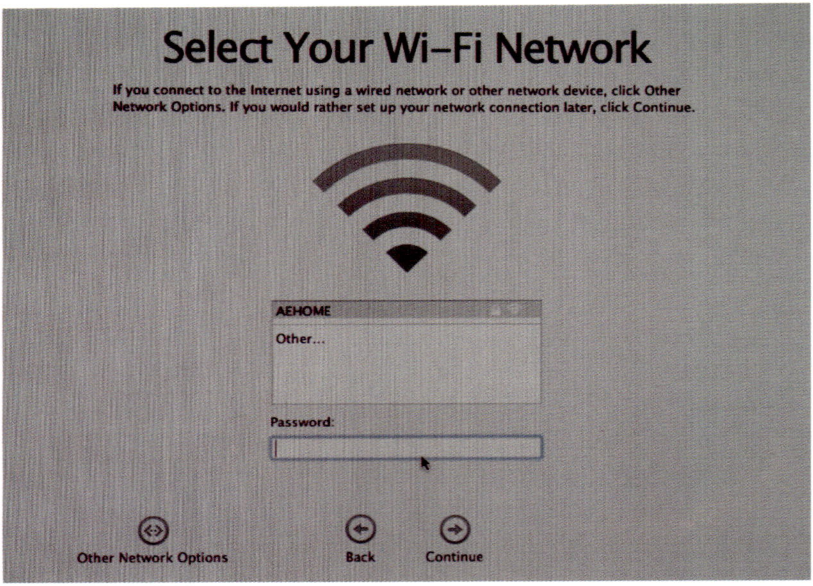

Figure 2-3 Selecting a wireless network

> You don't have to join a wireless network now, or if you are not at home when you are setting up your Mac you can easily do it later. For more on this see Chapter 5.

5. If you don't want to connect now just click on Other Network Options and select 'My computer does not connect to the Internet', as shown in Figure 2-4, and click Continue.

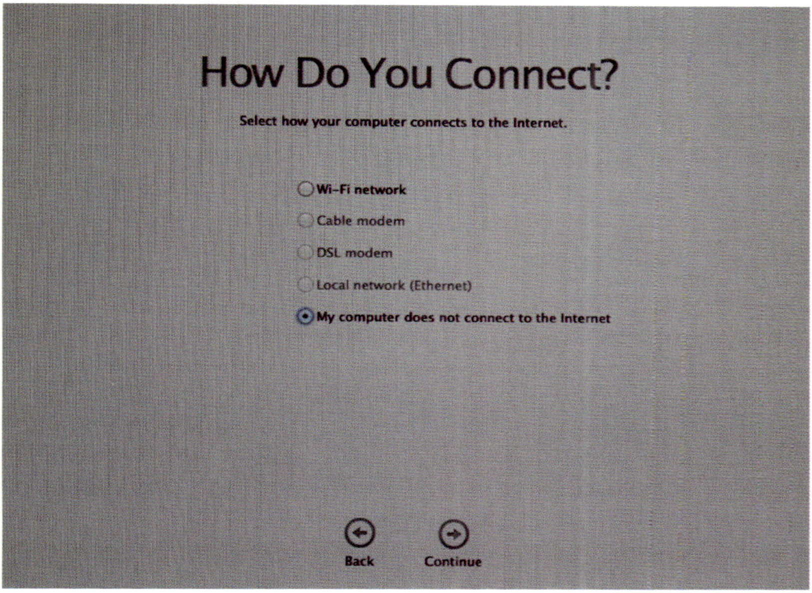

Figure 2-4 Choosing the Internet connection method

6. If you already own a Mac then you can now choose to transfer your information, as shown in Figure 2-5, otherwise ensure 'Not Now' is selected, then click Continue.

> If you are performing a new installation but you want to restore your existing programs, settings and files from a Time Machine backup, you can select that from here. To learn more about Time Machine, see Chapter 8.

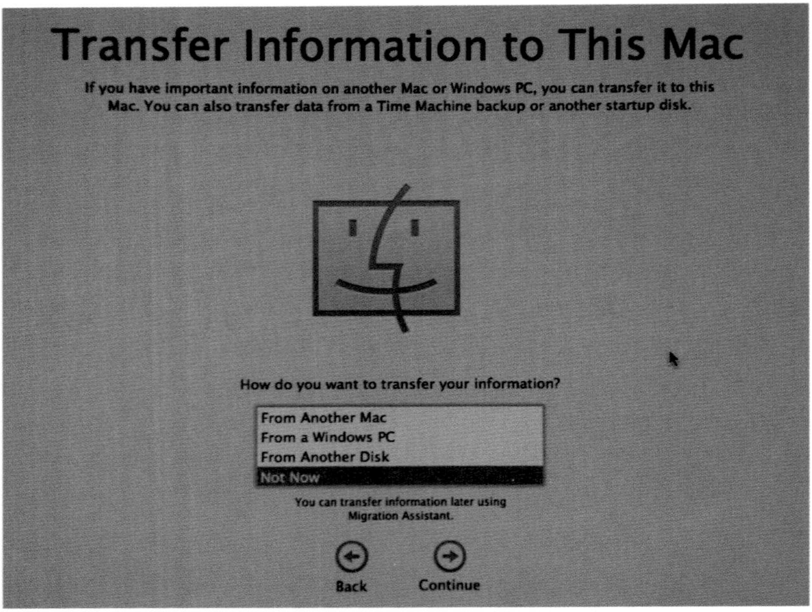

Figure 2-5 Choosing a transfer option

7. Read the Terms and Conditions and click Continue.
8. Next it's time to create your user account. Enter the following details:
    a. your name
    b. account name
    c. password (and then enter it again to verify it)
    d. password hint

    as shown in Figure 2-6, then click Continue.

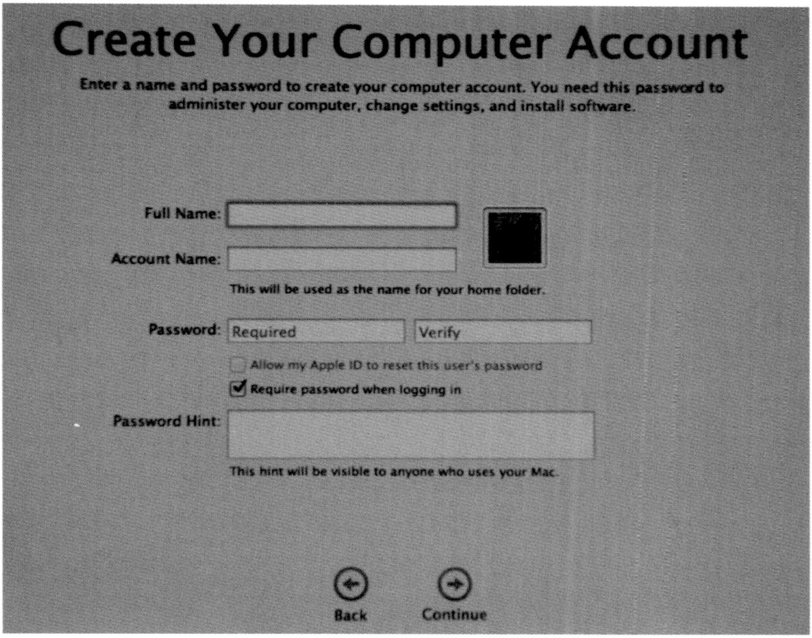

Figure 2-6 Creating your user account

9. Select your time zone by either clicking on the map or selecting the closest city from the drop-down list, as shown in Figure 2-7. Then click Continue.

Figure 2-7 Selecting your time zone

10. To continue, click Start using your Mac.

And that's it – you have now performed the initial set-up for your Mac and created your user account.

Summary

In this chapter you have learnt about the steps needed to complete the initial set-up of your new Mac. In the next chapter we will take a look at the Desktop and how to use your Mac.

3

The Mac Desktop

In this chapter we will take a look at the Mac Desktop, explaining the layout and where things are, and how to do everyday things, including emptying the trash and shutting down your Mac.

A Look at the Desktop

The first time you see the Mac desktop, you will notice just how clean and uncluttered it is, as you can see in Figure 3-1.

The desktop is split up into multiple areas – the main desktop window, the menu bar and the dock.

Everything you need to do with your Mac can be accessed and controlled from here, just as you would expect.

> You can personalise the look and feel of the desktop to meet your own requirements. Take a look at the next chapter to see how to do this.

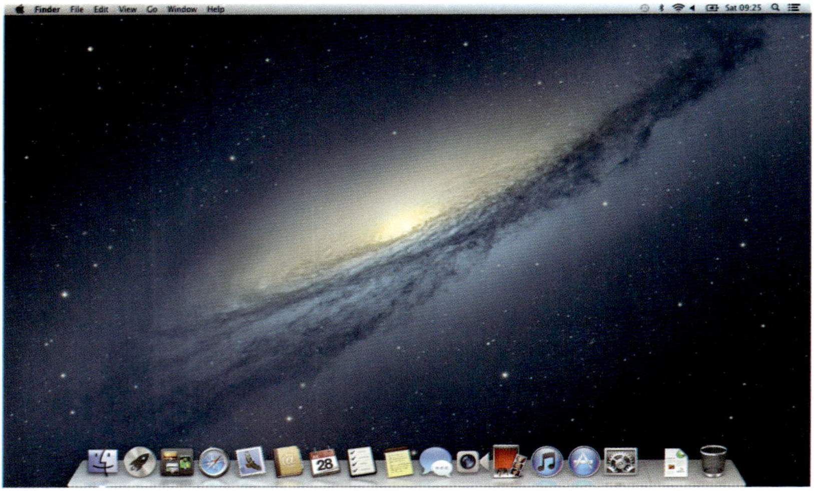

Figure 3-1 The Mac Desktop

The Menu Bar

The Menu Bar goes across the whole of the top of the screen and is split into two sections. The section on the left, as shown in Figure 3-2, contains various menu items, including the Apple menu accessed by clicking on the Apple icon and various other options, including access Help.

Figure 3-2 The Menu Bar (Left section)

When you are in an application, the menu items will change to give application-specific options. You will also be able to see which application you are in, as the name of that application appears to the right of the Apple logo (so in the example in Figure 3-2, the application is Finder).

The section on the right, as shown in Figure 3-3, contains various items that give you information, such as date and time, if you are connected to a wireless network, sounds, battery life and more. If you are used to Windows, then this is the sort of information that would appear in the system tray.

Figure 3-3 Menu Bar (Right section)

Finder

Finder allows you to manage files, folders, disks and more.

The Finder icon is the one that looks like a face, as shown in Figure 3-4.

Figure 3-4 Finder

When you click in Finder it opens up the view shown in Figure 3-5.

You will see in the left column (known as the Sidebar) there are a number of sections, including:

- FAVORITES: here you can access places such as your desktop and various folders.
- DEVICES: here you will be able to access any devices, such as your hard drive

Figure 3-5 A view in Finder

> You can easily change the view in Finder as well by clicking on one of the four view icons at the top of the screen, as shown in Figure 3-6. The choice is down to personal preference so check each of them out and decide which you like best.

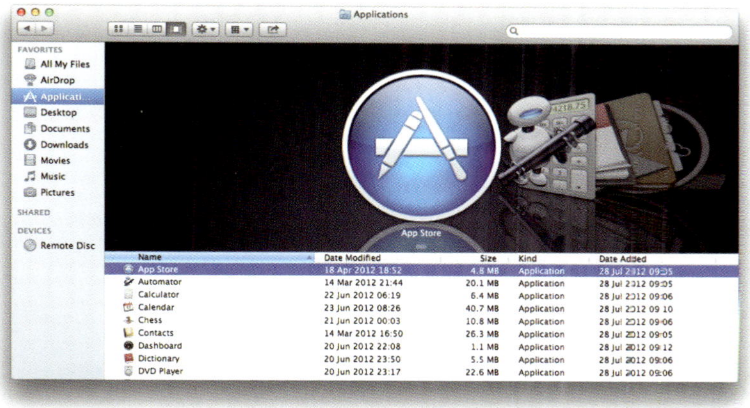

Figure 3-6 A different Finder view

You will see other information displayed here as well, such as the date added, shown in the right column in Figure 3-6.

There are also a number of different settings and preferences you can set with Finder, for example what window Finder will open in, and what items you want to appear in the sidebar.

To change these preferences:

1. When Finder is open, click on Finder in the menu bar and select Preferences.
2. The General tab will be displayed, as shown in Figure 3-7.

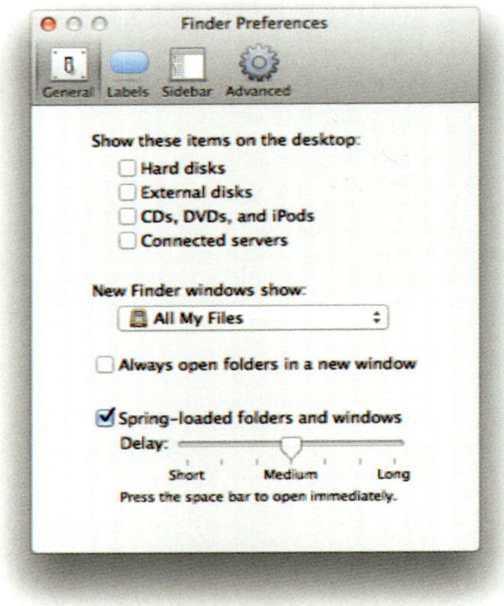

Figure 3-7 Finder Preference – General

3. You can now make changes here as you see fit.
4. To change the items shown in the Sidebar, click the Sidebar tab.
5. You will now see the list of current items, as shown in Figure 3-8. If you want to remove any, just click on them to remove the tick.

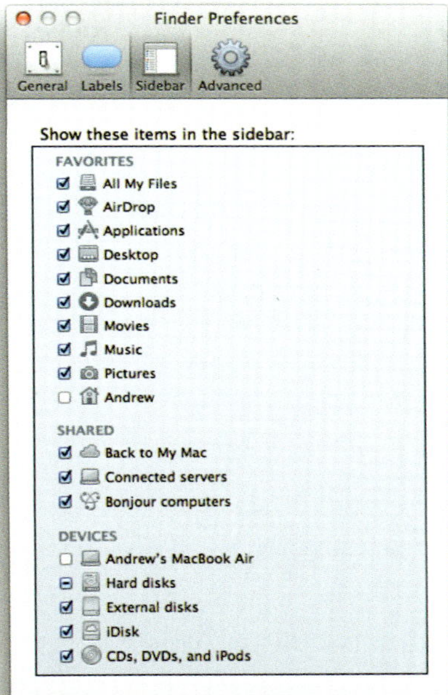

Figure 3-8 Finder Preferences

Finder will take a little time to get used to, especially if you are used to Windows, but stick with it, and eventually you will wonder how you got on without it.

The Dock

The Dock, which by default appears at the bottom of the screen – as shown in Figure 3-9, provides quick access to applications and folders.

Figure 3-9 The Dock

If you click on an application in the Dock it will start. That application's icon will then show a blue dot under it to show you that it is currently running.

> Unlike Windows, when you close a Mac window it doesn't quit the application. Go into each application and quit the application via the Menu bar. If you don't quit applications then you will quickly run out of system resources as each open application will use valuable resources.

If a folder is in the Dock, such as the applications folder and you click on it, it will either open the folder to show its contents, or it will open in an arc to show items you can select. Either way these groups of applications and folders are known as Stacks. The default stacks are: Applications, Documents and Downloads. Why not click on them now to have a look at what they contain?

There are a number of applications in the Dock when you first start, but you can easily add or remove those applications.

To add an application to the Dock:

1. Find the application that you want to add to the Dock.
2. Drag the application to the left of the Dock's separator line, as shown in Figure 3-10.

Figure 3-10 The Dock Separator line

To add a document or folder to the Dock:

1. Find the document or folder that you want to add to the Dock.
2. Drag the document or folder to the right of the Dock's separator line.

> If there are applications on the Dock that you don't use very often, or at all, you should remove them to make it cleaner and easier to use, and give you more space for those you do.

The Trash

When you want to remove a file or an application from your Mac, you first place it in the Trash (it's the same as the Recycle Bin in Windows).

To put something in the Trash:

1. There are a couple of different ways to put something in the Trash. Either drag and drop it into the Trash on the Dock (last icon on the right), or right click on the item, as shown in Figure 3-11.

Figure 3-11 Moving something to the Trash

2. Click on ‘Move to Trash’.

If you accidentally move something to the Trash you want to get back it is very simple to do:

1. Click on the Trash to open and reveal the contents.
2. Locate the file or files you want to recover.
3. Either drag them to your desktop, or right-click on them and select ‘Put Back’, as shown in Figure 3-12 to place them where they were before you deleted them.

Figure 3-12 Recovering something from the Trash

In order to save disk space, you should regularly empty the Trash. To do this:

1. Right-click on the Trash icon.

2. Click 'Empty Trash', as shown in Figure 3-13.

Figure 3-13 Emptying the Trash

If you want to erase the files so that they can never be recovered, even with specialist software, there is a feature called Secure Empty Trash. Files deleted in this way are completely overwritten by meaningless data. If you press the Command key after right-clicking the Trash, you can then select 'Secure Empty Trash' as shown in Figure 3-14.

Figure 3-14 Securely emptying the Trash

3. You will need to confirm that you want to empty the Trash, as shown in Figure 3-15.

> Once the Trash has been emptied, anything in there will be gone, so make sure that you really want to empty the trash before continuing.

Figure 3-15 Confirming the trash emptying

Shutting Down Your Mac

There will come a time when you want to shut down your Mac (or even do a restart).

> Do not just press and hold the power button to shut down as this could result in corrupt files.

Doing so is simple:

1. Click on the Apple icon (see Figure 3-2).
2. Choose 'Shut Down' (or Restart) from the menu, as shown in Figure 3-16.

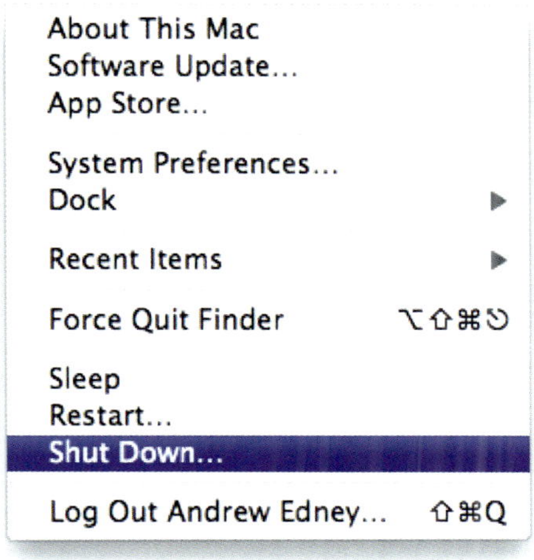

Figure 3-16 Shutting Down

> Instead of shutting down your Mac, why not just put it to sleep? This way it will start up faster and you can leave applications open ready for you to use. If you have a MacBook Air this process is instant and just involves closing and opening the screen!

Controlling Windows

No, not THAT Windows! Whenever you open a folder, the contents are displayed in a window. You can control the position of the window by dragging it to wherever you want on the desktop. You can also control the size of the window by clicking and dragging the bottom right corner of the window.

You will also notice that in the top left corner of every window are three coloured buttons, as shown in Figure 3-17.

Figure 3-17 Window buttons

They function as follows:

- Red: Close the window
- Yellow: Minimise the window
- Green: Maximise the window

> When you minimise a window, it will automatically be placed in the Dock, making it easy to open again when you need it.

Using any of these, or any combination of these makes it very easy to control just how you want to see windows on the Mac.

Summary

In this chapter you have learnt about the Mac desktop, and how to do a few things. Before you go any further you should take some time to play around with the various features mentioned in the chapter so that you can get used to them. And don't worry, some of them do take a little getting used to. In the next chapter we will take a look at how you can personalise your Mac.

4

Personalising Your Mac

In this chapter we will take a look at how you can customise and personalise the desktop to make it your own, changing things from the colour used, to the desktop image and even adding a photo screen saver. We will also show you how to conserve battery life and make changes to the Mac's energy settings.

Changing the Desktop Image

If you decide that you don't want to keep the default desktop image (called Galaxy – personally I quite like it), you can easily change it to one of the others that Apple provide, or you can add one of your own.

To change the desktop image:

1. Click on the Apple icon.
2. Click on 'System Preferences' from the drop-down list.

3. Click on the Desktop & Screen Saver icon from the Personal area, as shown in Figure 4-1.

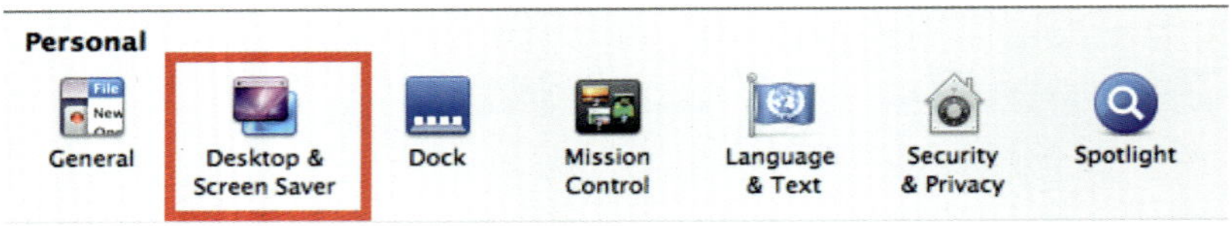

Figure 4-1 The Personal area in System Preferences

4. Click on the Desktop tab to display the various choices, as shown in Figure 4-2.

Figure 4-2 Changing the desktop picture

5. Work through the various images and see if there is one you like. Click on it to have it change immediately.

6. If you want to use your own image, click on the + sign then locate your chosen image, as shown in Figure 4-3.

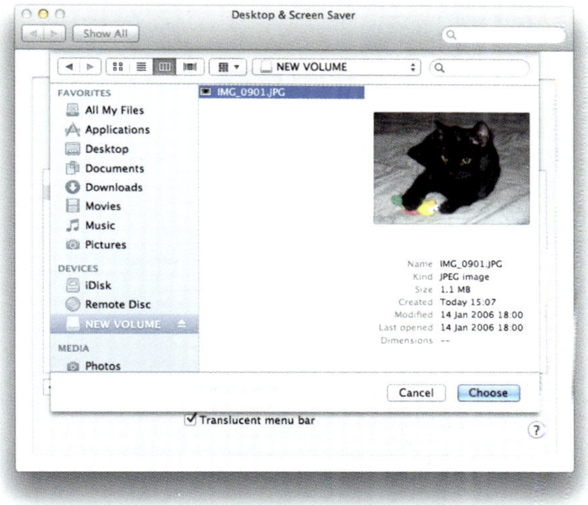

Figure 4-3 Using a background of your own

7. Then click on the Choose button to use it and your desktop image will be personal just to you, as shown in Figure 4-4.

> If you want to be a little different, you can have the desktop image change on a regular basis and even set the time. This can be fun, but also a little distracting!

Figure 4-4 The new background

> A quick way to use a picture as a desktop image is to right-click on an image and select 'Set Desktop Picture' from anywhere on your Mac.

Changing the Screen Saver

While you are in the Desktop and Screen Saver window, why not change the screen saver to something else, for example, a selection of your favourite photos?

To change the screen saver:

1. Click on the Screen Saver tab on the Desktop & Screen Saver window, as shown in Figure 4-2.

2. By default, the screen saver is set to Computer Name, as shown in Figure 4-5. You can now select any of the other screen savers from the list, or if you have pictures on your Mac you can select an image source to have as your screen saver.

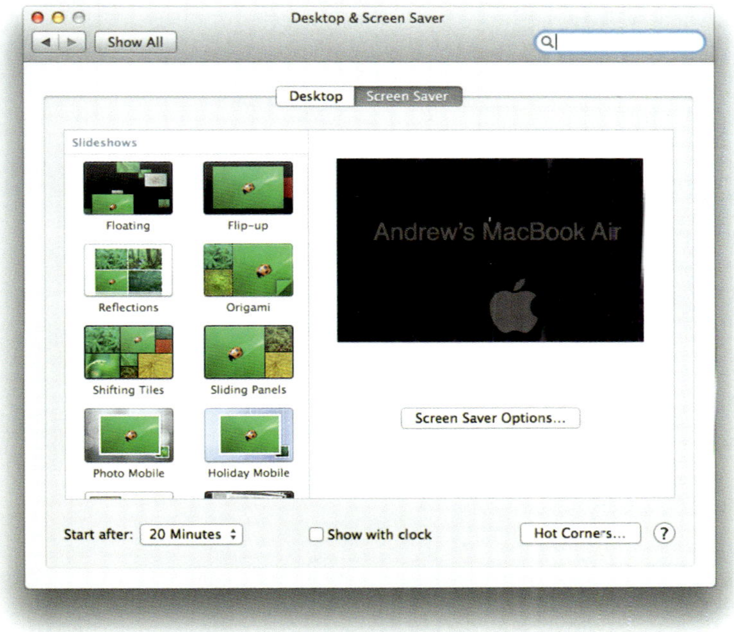

Figure 4-5 Changing the screen saver

3. Some of the screen saver selections have the ability to set specific options. If you want to view and change these, click on the Screen Saver Options button after

you have selected a screen saver (if given the opportunity).

4. Use the 'Start after' drop-down box to set the number of minutes before the screen saver kicks-in.

> Make sure that your energy-saving preference setting is longer than the amount of time before the screen saver kicks-in otherwise you will never see it as your Mac will go into power save mode!

Changing the Appearance

Now that you have changed the desktop image and set a screen saver, you can also change various other appearance settings, including the colour of buttons and the number of items that can appear in the recent items list.

To make appearance changes:

1. Click on the Apple icon.
2. Click on 'System Preferences' from the drop-down list.
3. From the Personal area, click on the General icon.
4. Make any changes to the appearance that you want, as shown in Figure 4-6.

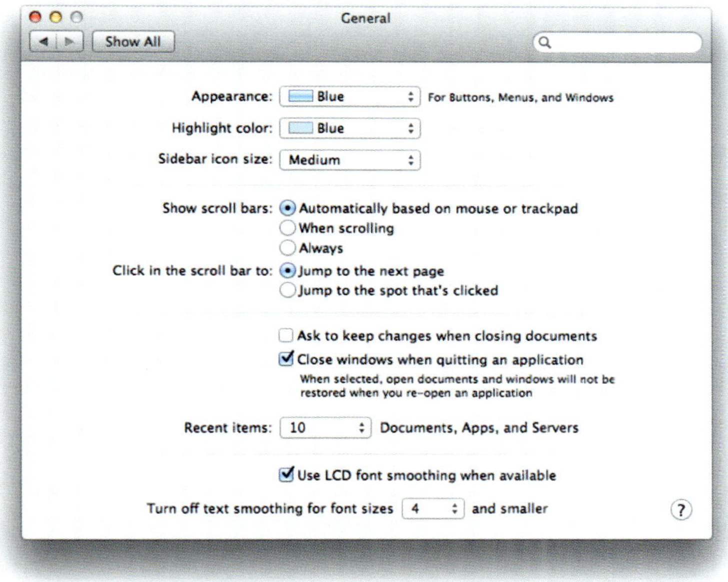

Figure 4-6 Changing your Mac appearance settings

> If you want to find out more about each specific setting, click on the question mark in the bottom right corner of the Appearance window.

Try out a few different settings to see which you like best.

Personalising the Dock

You can also change the look and feel of the Dock if you so wish. For example, if you don't like the Dock being at the bottom of the screen, how about on the left or right instead? Or would you like the icons in the Dock to be bigger (or smaller for that matter)?

To personalise the Dock:

1. Click on the Dock icon from the Personal area of System Preferences.
2. Make any changes you wish, as shown in Figure 4-7.

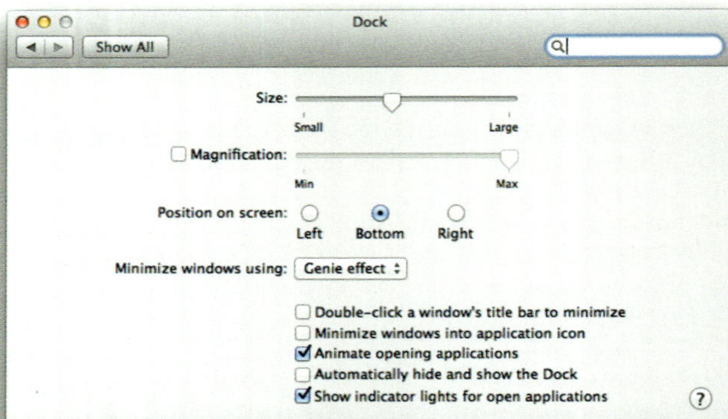

Figure 4-7 Personalising the Dock

You can also make changes to the Dock by clicking on the Apple logo and selecting 'Dock' from the drop-down list.

One of the nicer features you can enable is Magnification. When enabled, any icon in the Dock you move your pointer over will be magnified, as shown in Figure 4-8, making it easier to see and select. This is very useful if you have a lot of things in your Dock.

Figure 4-8 Magnifying parts of the Dock

One of the settings I personally like to use is the 'Automatically hide and show the Dock' option. What this does is hide the Dock when it is not in use, giving you more screen area to view and then making the Dock reappear when you move your pointer to the bottom of the screen. Give it a try and see what you think.

Conserving Battery Life

If you are running on the battery, rather than being connected to a power source, then you will want to get as much time as possible out of that battery charge.

You can conserve battery life by setting a time limit when the Mac will be put into sleep mode or when the display will sleep (when you are not actually doing anything on the Mac).

To make changes, do the following:

1. Click on the Apple icon.
2. Click on System Preferences.
3. Click on the Energy Saver icon from the Hardware area, as shown in Figure 4-9.

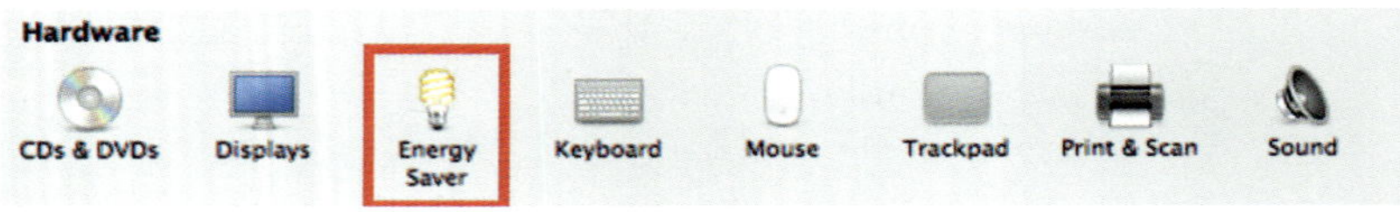

Figure 4-9 Launching Energy Saver

4. Click on the Battery tab to display the specific settings when using the Mac only on battery power, as shown in Figure 4-10.
5. Using the sliders, set the time parameters for when the Mac will sleep and when the screen will sleep.
6. You can also make similar settings for when the Mac is running on mains power by clicking on the 'Power Adapter' tab and performing the same steps.

> By default the battery status is shown in the menu bar. I would recommend leaving this enabled so that you can see how much battery life you have when running on batteries, or how long it will take until the Mac is fully charged if you are connected to a power source.

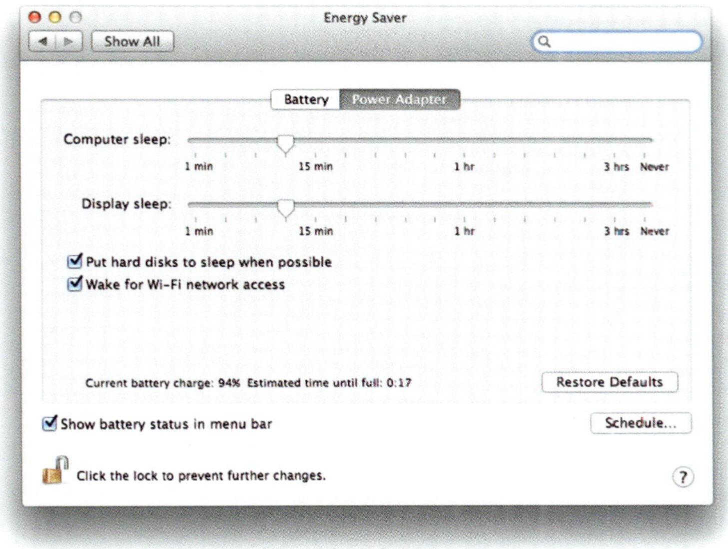

Figure 4-10 Making changes to the Energy settings

By default, when you are on battery power you will see a battery icon that gradually changes showing the reduction in battery charge. While it is good to see how much power you have left, it isn't very accurate. You can choose to change this to include the percentage of battery left (although that still doesn't give you an exact idea, but it's better than nothing).

To change the battery icon:

1. Click on the battery icon from the menu bar.

2. Click on 'Show Percentage' from the drop-down menu, as shown in Figure 4-11.

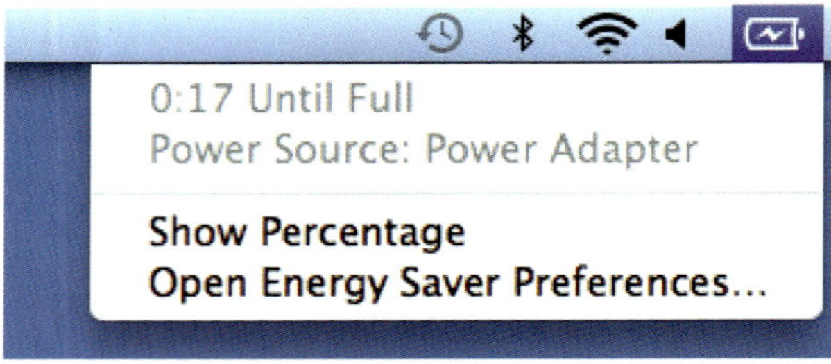

Figure 4-11 Changing how the power is displayed

The amount of battery power remaining in percentage is only an estimate based on your current usage. This will be continually updated, so don't rely on having that amount if you plan on doing something more battery intensive.

Changing the Clock

One other setting that a lot of people change to suit their preference is the clock. The default option is to show the day of the week and a digital readout of the time.

To change these settings:

1. From the System Preference window, click on 'Date & Time' in the System area.
2. Click on the Clock tab to display the various options shown in Figure 4-12.

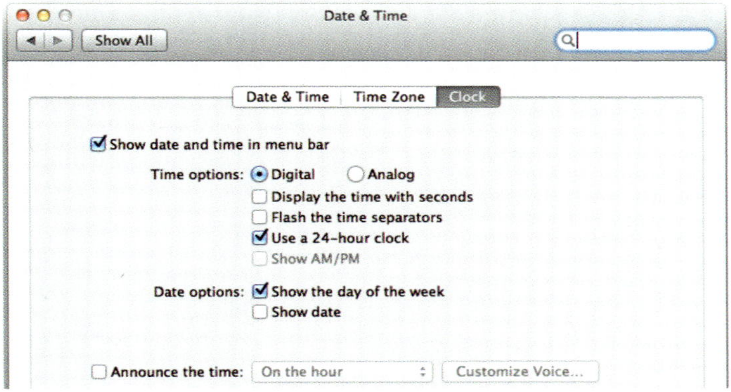

Figure 4-12 Changing the clock settings

3. Make your changes by clicking on the various options.

> You can also change the date or time itself by clicking on the Date & Time tab. You should also tick the box marked 'Set date and time automatically' so whenever the clocks change you will have the correct time on your Mac.

Notifications

Notifications are new feature with Mountain Lion. If you have used an iPhone or iPad you might be familiar with them.

Notifications are alerts that appear in the upper-right of your screen without interrupting what you are doing.

You can add and remove applications from the Notification Center and even decide on the style of the alert you want to receive.

To make changes to the Notification Center:

1. From the System Preference window, click on 'Notifications' in the System area.
2. Click on the apps to display the various options shown in Figure 4-13.

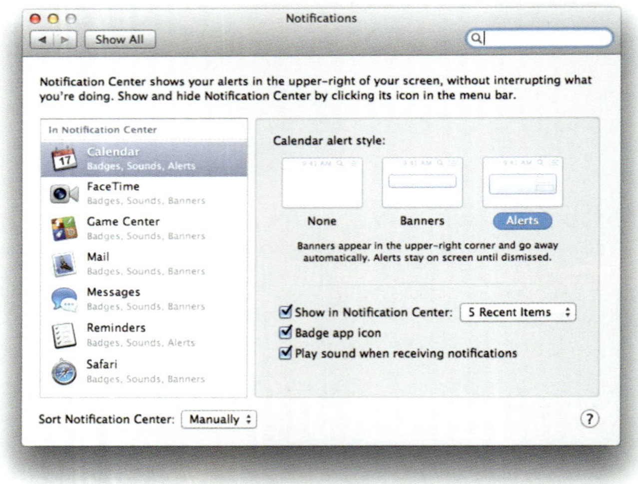

Figure 4-13 Notifications

Summary

In this chapter you have learnt how to make some changes to the desktop, and your Mac, in order to personalise your Mac user experience. In the next chapter we will take a look at connecting your Mac to your network.

5

Connecting to Your Network

In this chapter we will look at how to connect your MacBook to your home network, how to use wi-fi and, also, how to connect your MacBook to a printer either directly or over the network.

Connecting to a Network

If you connect to a network using an Ethernet cable and your Mac has an Ethernet port, then all you have to do is plug in the cable and that's it.

Using Wireless to Connect

It is more than likely that the majority of the time, if not all of the time, you want to connect to a wireless network.

Connecting to a wireless network is very easy, you just need the network name and password.

The one thing you should always be mindful of is the wireless network itself. If you are in your home or office then you have some level of confidence in using it. However if you are out and about and find "free wi-fi" you should always be careful when using it, especially when using your credit card or anything that requires a password, which could be captured.

To connect to a wireless network:

1. On the top bar click on the Wireless icon, as shown in Figure 5-1.

Figure 5-1 The Wireless icon

2. Ensure the Wi-Fi is On (if it is off just click on Turn Wi-Fi On) and locate the wireless network you want to connect to from the network list as shown in Figure 5-2, and click on it – for example, AEHOME is the network that I want to connect to, so I just click on it.

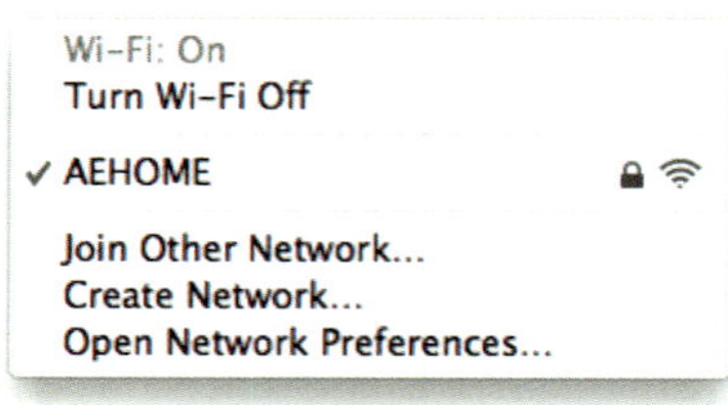

Figure 5-2 Selecting a wireless network

3. As this network is protected (as most wireless networks are, or should be) type in the network password into the box shown in Figure 5-3 and click Join.

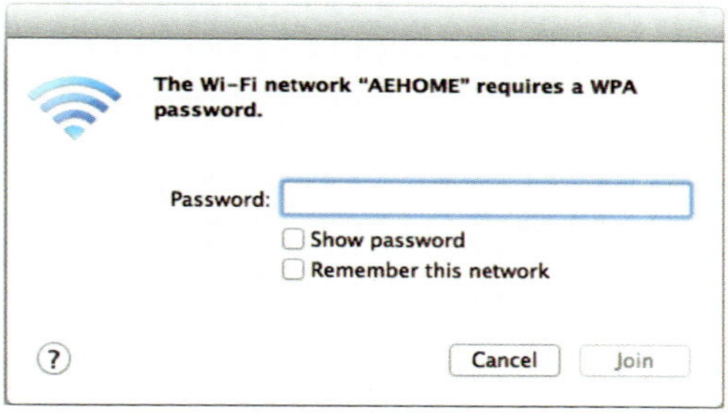

Figure 5-3 Enter the wireless network password

> If you are going to connect to this particular wireless network on a regular basis, say for example because it is your home network, you should ensure the 'Remember this network' box is ticked so that you won't have to keep connecting manually to the network each time.

And that's it – you are now connected, so you can surf away, although you should read the next chapter on Securing Your Mac before you do any surfing!

Using the Network Setup Assistant

If you are not sure about connecting to a wireless network using the method from the previous section, there is a built-in Network Setup Assistant to help you make the connection.

To use the Network Setup Assistant:

1. From the menu bar click on the Wireless icon.
2. Ensure the Wi-Fi is On (if it is off just click on Turn Wi-Fi On) and then click on 'Open Network Preferences'.
3. This will display the Network page, as shown in Figure 5-4. From here you can see that the Wi-Fi is On. So just click on the 'Assist me' button to continue.

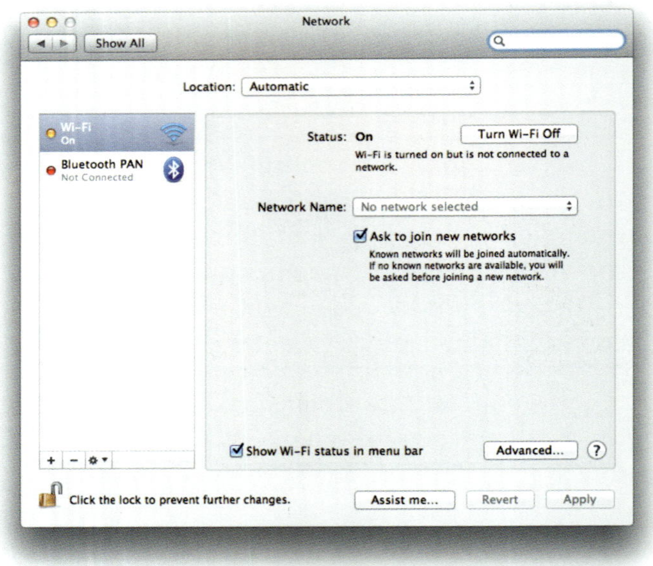

Figure 5-4 Network options

4. You will be asked if you want assistance, as shown in Figure 5-5, which you do, so click on Assistant to continue.

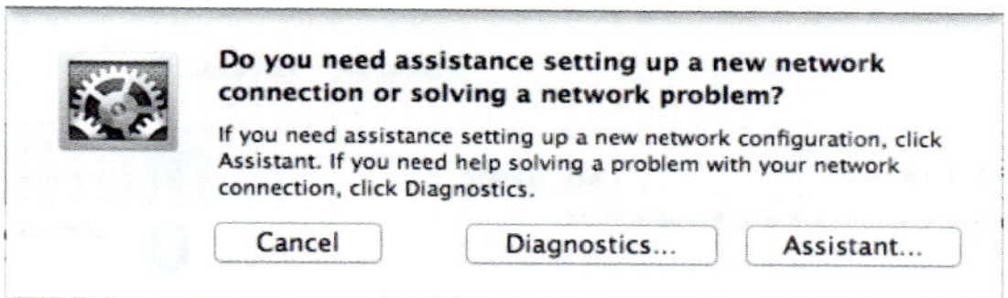

Figure 5-5 Do you need assistance?

5. Next you create a network location name, so type something in the box shown in Figure 5-6. Don't leave the default in as it isn't very useful as you can see, so put in a description like "home" or "office" or something along those lines, then click Continue.

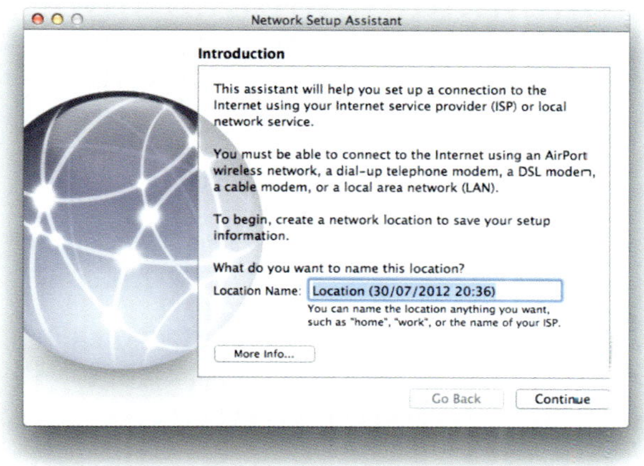

Figure 5-6 Naming the network location

6. Choose how you want to connect to the Internet, as shown in Figure 5-7. In my case, I only have AirPort operational so I can only select that option. Then click Continue.

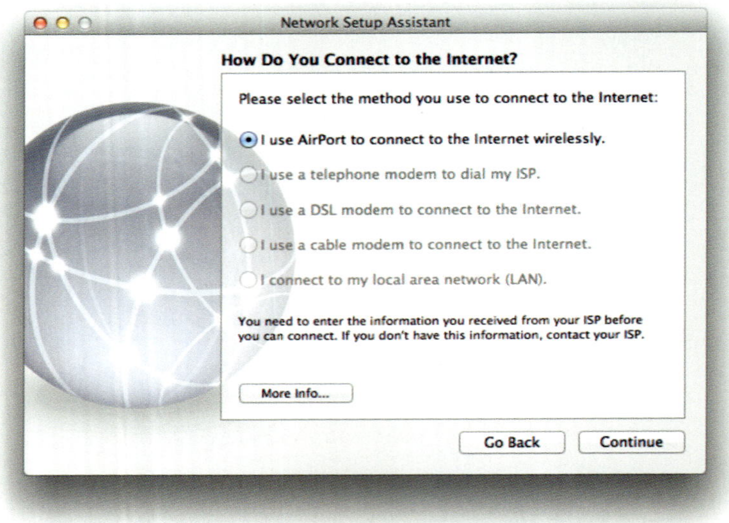

Figure 5-7 Choosing how you connect to the Internet

7. The list of available wireless networks will then be displayed, as shown in Figure 5-8. Just click on the one you want to connect to and then type in the network password and click Continue.

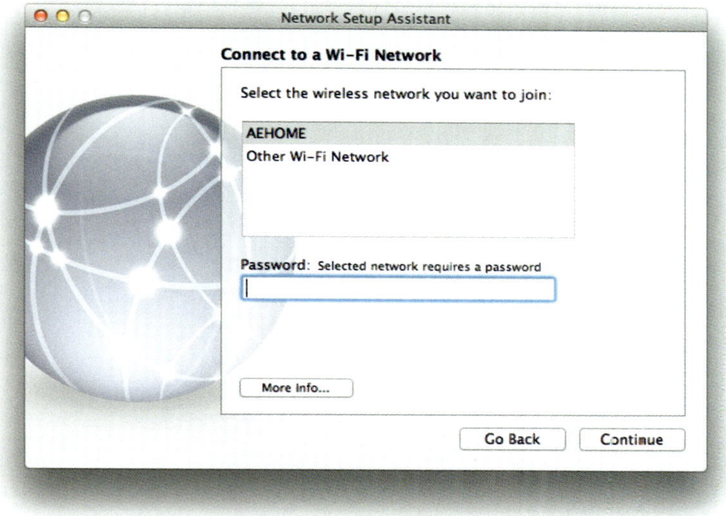

Figure 5-8 Selecting your wireless network

> If the wireless network you want to connect to is not displayed in the list, check that the wireless network is broadcasting.

8. You will then be asked if you are ready to connect, as shown in Figure 5-9. So click Continue to connect.

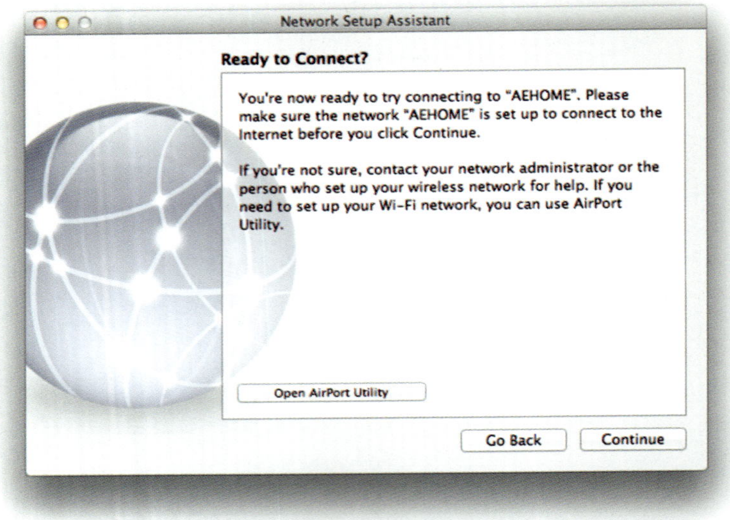

Figure 5-9 Are you ready to connect?

9. You should now be connected to the network, as shown in Figure 5-10. So just click Done and away you go.

> As we mentioned earlier, before you do any surfing on the Internet you should take a look at the next chapter on how to secure your Mac.

Figure 5-10 You are now connected

Connecting to a Printer

If you want to connect to a printer and use it to print, you have to first add it to the Mac and download the correct printer driver.

To do this:

1. Click on the Apple logo and then click on System Preferences.
2. From the Hardware area, click on Print & Scan, as shown in Figure 5-11.

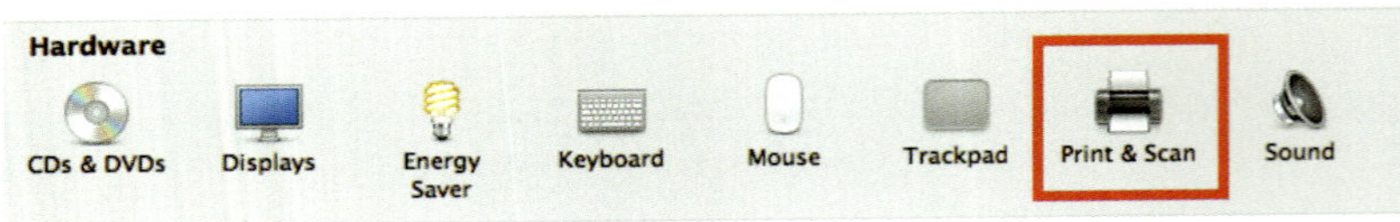

Figure 5-11 Selecting the Print & Scan icon

3. You will then see the list of connected available printers, as shown in Figure 5-12. In my case I don't currently have any added. Click on the + button to start the adding process and select 'Add Other Printer or Scanner'.

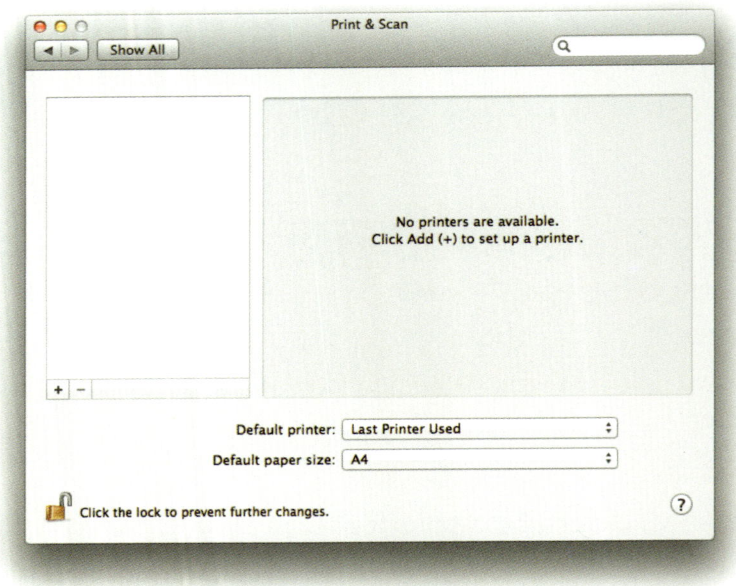

Figure 5-12 Viewing Print & Scan

4. The list of available printers, both directly connected to the Mac and those on your network (either wired or wireless) should then be displayed, as shown in Figure 5-13. Click on the printer you want to use and then click Add.

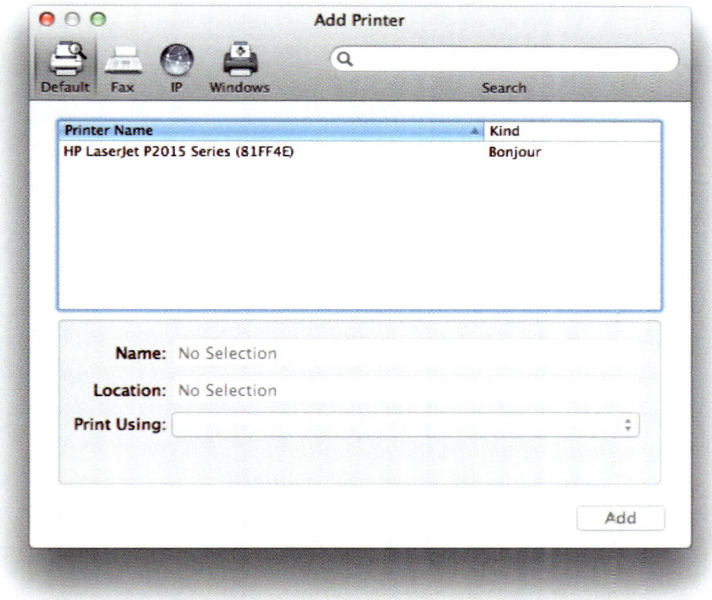

Figure 5-13 Adding a printer

> You must be connected to the Internet for this part of the process as your Mac will connect to the Apple website and download the correct drivers for you. If there are no drivers available you should contact the manufacturer of the printer you want to connect to and check if they support the Mac.

5. The driver software will now be downloaded and installed. You can see the progress, as shown in Figure 5-14. Remember to be patient as the driver size might be quite large.

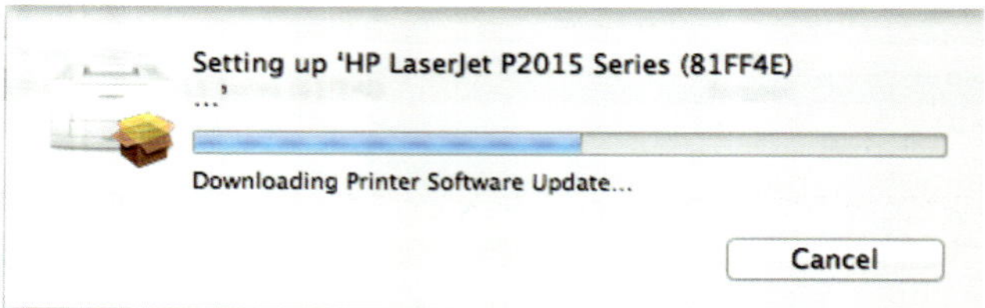

Figure 5-14 Waiting for the software to download and install

6. After the driver has been successfully installed, you will see the printer shown on the Print & Scan page, as shown in Figure 5-15.

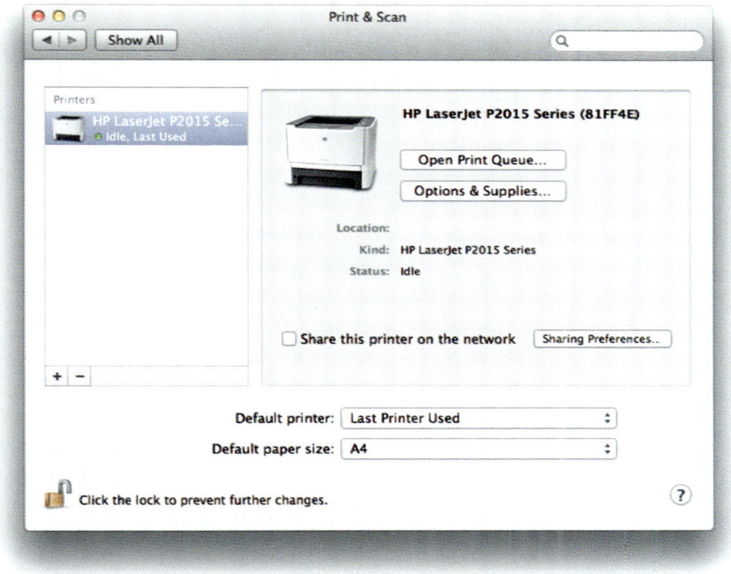

Figure 5-15 Details on your installed printer

You can also check printer settings and supply levels by clicking on the Options & Supplies button.

You can now print from any application on your Mac that supports printing.

Summary

In this chapter you have learnt how to connect your Mac to a wired and a wireless network. You have also learnt how to connect to a printer in order to print from supported applications. In the next chapter you will learn how to secure your Mac in order to help protect you and your data.

6

Securing Your Mac

Securing your Mac is probably one of the most important steps you will take when first setting everything up. This step includes setting up a password for your user account, enabling the firewall to protect you when you are online, protecting yourself against viruses and keeping your MacBook updated with any security fixes and updates.

> Do not skip this chapter or these steps. They are extremely important and will protect both you and your MacBook.
>
> **Don't say I didn't warn you!**

Setting a Password

It is a very good idea to set a password for your user account. This stops other people from gaining access to your MacBook and, also, making changes to your settings. If you have already set a password for your account during the initial setup you can skip this section.

If you didn't, or you want to change your password, follow these steps:

1. Click on the Apple logo at the top of the screen and then click on System Preferences.
2. Click on the Users & Groups icon from the System area, as shown in Figure 6-1.

Figure 6-1 Select Users & Groups from System

3. Click on the Change Password as shown in Figure 6-2.

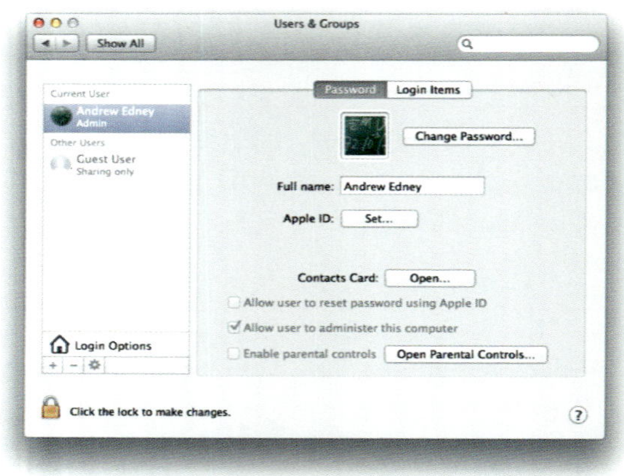

Figure 6-2 The Users & Groups window

4. Type in the password you want to use in the boxes and enter a password hint, as shown in Figure 6-3.

> Do not make your password easy to guess. Steer clear of your favourite pets name, or your children, or something really obvious. And if you do enter a password hint, make sure it is something only you will recognise.

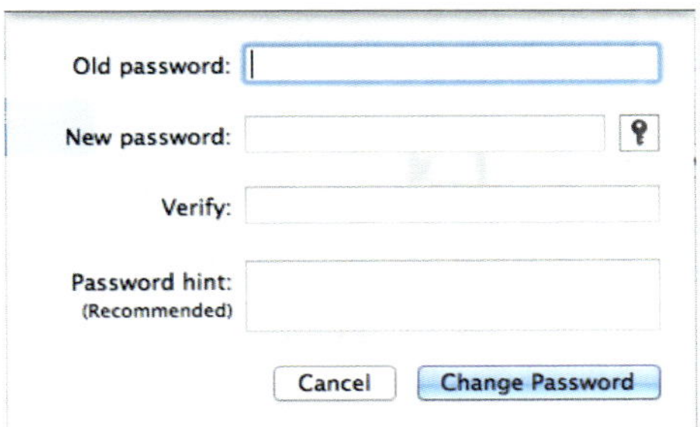

Figure 6-3 Setting a password and hint

5. Click the Change Password button, and then click OK.

Enabling the Firewall

You may be asking yourself "what is a firewall?" Simply put, a firewall is a piece of software (or hardware) that is used to protect your MacBook or network from outside sources. You can allow certain applications (such as the Internet or Email) through the firewall, and have everything else stopped.

A firewall is a very good idea, as it will help protect you against attacks from the Internet and other networks that your MacBook might be connected to.

Your MacBook has a built-in software application firewall, which allows you to control connections on a per-application basis, rather than a per-port basis. This makes it easier to gain the benefits of firewall protection, and helps prevent undesirable applications from taking control of network ports that have been opened for legitimate applications.

But it isn't enabled by default, which has always struck me as a strange move on the part of Apple. There is no logical reason why you would not want to enable the firewall. Don't worry though, it is very simple to enable, just follow these steps:

1. Click on the Apple logo at the top of the screen and then click on System Preferences.
2. Click on the Security & Privacy icon from the Personal area, as shown in Figure 6-4.

Figure 6-4 System Preferences

3. Click on the Firewall tab.
4. To enable the firewall, just click on the Turn On Firewall button, as shown in Figure 6-5.

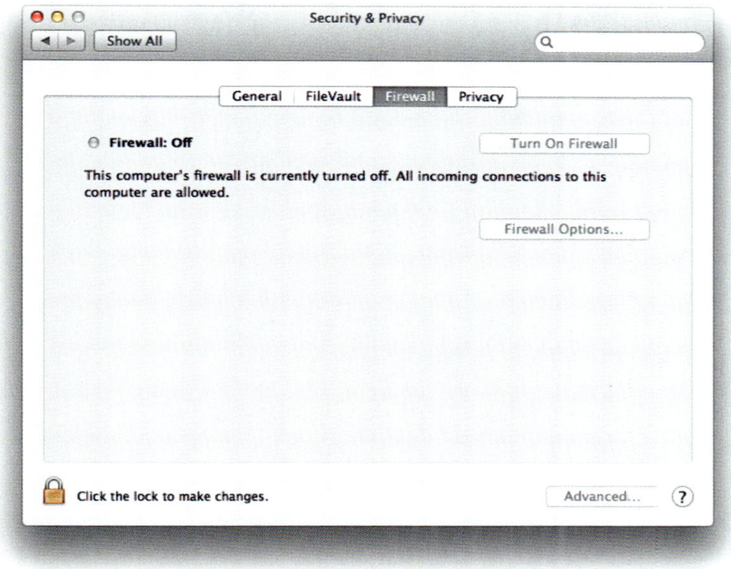

Figure 6-5 Turning on the Firewall

> If you cannot start the firewall, you might have to click the padlock to open it and allow changes to be made. In the figure above changes cannot be made as the padlock is closed.

5. You then need to select how you want the firewall to perform, so click on the Firewall Options button.

Once enabled, by default, the firewall is set to 'Automatically allow signed software to receive incoming connections', as shown in Figure 6-6.

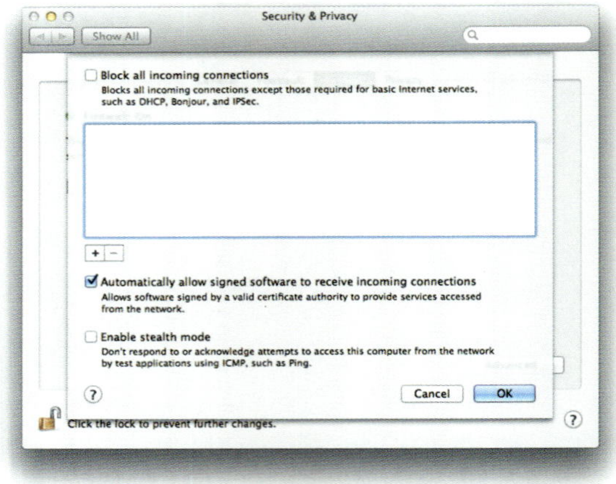

Figure 6-6 Selecting the firewall mode

6. If you want to be really secure, check the 'Block all incoming connections' box.

> The 'Automatically allow signed software to receive incoming connections' setting is the one you want if you want to use software such as Skype for making voice and video calls. When you install a recognised software program it will automatically be added to the allowed connections list.

7. Click OK to close the window and click on the padlock again to prevent further changes.

Anti-Virus Software

You may have heard people say things like “Macs don’t get viruses”. Well unfortunately that just simply isn’t true. What is true is that Macs get ***less*** viruses than Windows, but a virus is a virus, and you don’t want to get one!

So, with that in mind you will need to get yourself some anti-virus software. The usual players, Norton, McAfee, Sophos, etc, produce software for the Mac, and Sophos in particular give it away for free.

You can download Sophos Anti-Virus for Mac Home Edition, as shown in Figure 6-7 from http://www.sophos.com/en-us/products/free-tools/sophos-antivirus-for-mac-home-edition.aspx

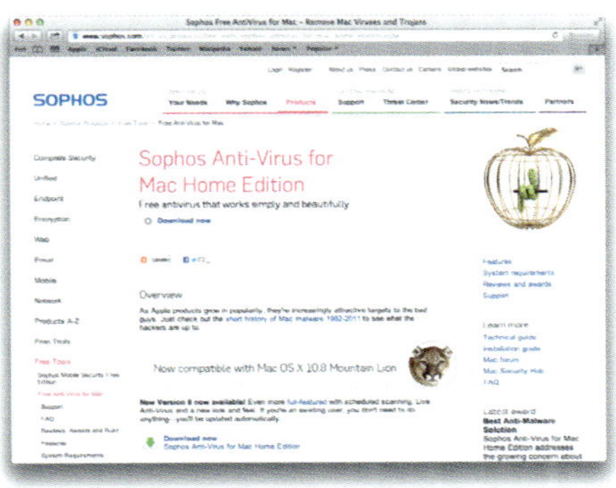

Figure 6-7 Finding Anti-Virus Software

> It is a good idea to run a regular anti-virus scan on your MacBook – say once a week. This ensures that there are no viruses present that may only have been discovered since the last anti-virus definition update.

Keeping your MacBook Updated

Like any other software, Apple often release updates for both the Mac operating system and for programs on the Mac. The updates can be program enhancement, bug fixes and often security updates.

> It is very important to check on a regular basis if there are any updates available, and if there are, install them as soon as possible, to ensure that your Mac is up to date and protected.

You can see what version of the OS you are currently running by clicking on the Apple icon and then clicking on About This Mac. This will show various information, including the version of the OS and processor and memory information, as shown in Figure 6-8.

To check for any available software updates, do the following:

1. Click on the Apple icon and then click on Software Update (or click Software Update from the About This Mac screen).

2. Wait while your Mac contacts Apple to check for any available software update. This process may take a few minutes, so be patient.

Figure 6-8 About This Mac

> It is always a good idea to check what the update is before installing it. This is to give you the choice of downloading and updating now, or doing it at a later time. For example, if the update was a 1.06GB system update, you might want to wait until you have more time.

3. Check through each of the displayed updates, as shown in Figure 6-9 and if you are happy to install them click on Update to begin.

> Depending on what the update is, you should consider saving anything you are working on prior to starting the update. This ensures that nothing you are working on is lost. Also, ensure that the MacBook is connected to a power supply to stop any problems with corrupted files if the MacBook runs out of battery power.

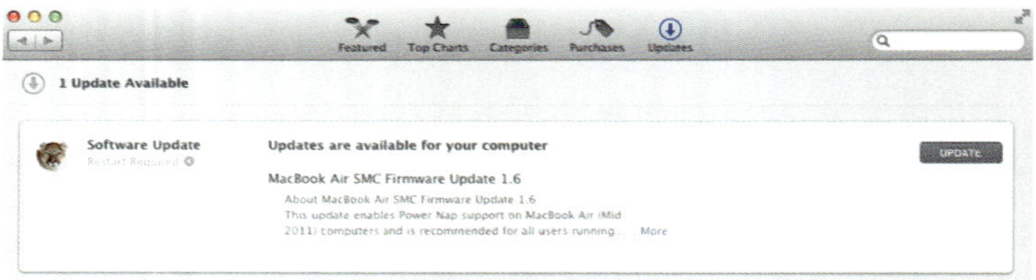

Figure 6-9 Choosing the updates to install

4. Sit back and wait for the updates to download and install.

5. If prompted, as shown in Figure 6-10, restart your MacBook.

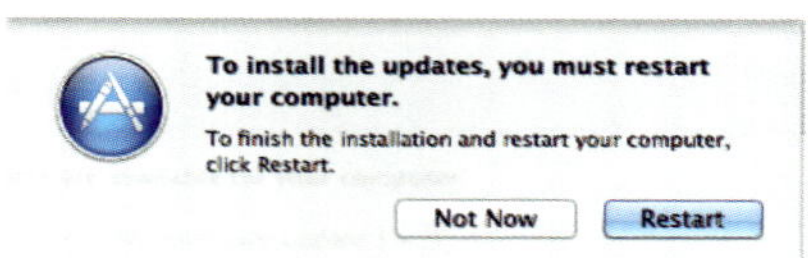

Figure 6-10 Restart your MacBook

Extra Protection

There are a couple of other things you can do to give yourself a little extra protection without much effort.

You can require the account password to be entered whenever the Mac wakes up from sleep and you can have your Mac log out after a set period of inactivity.

To use these just do the following:

1. Click on the Apple logo at the top of the screen and then click on System Preferences.
2. Click on the Security & Privacy icon from the Personal area.
3. Select the changes you want from the General tab, as shown in Figure 6-11.

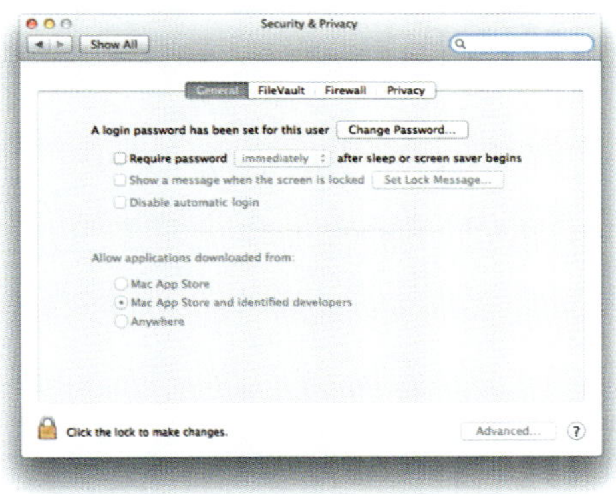

Figure 6-11 Making additional security changes

You may also have noticed the second tab – called FileVault. FileVault is used to encrypt the contents of your home folder, which means that if you switch it on then only your account will have access to the decrypted contents of that folder, giving you an extra layer of protection.

To enable FileVault:

1. Click on Security & Privacy from System Preferences.
2. Click on the FileVault tab to display the FileVault options, as shown in Figure 6-12.

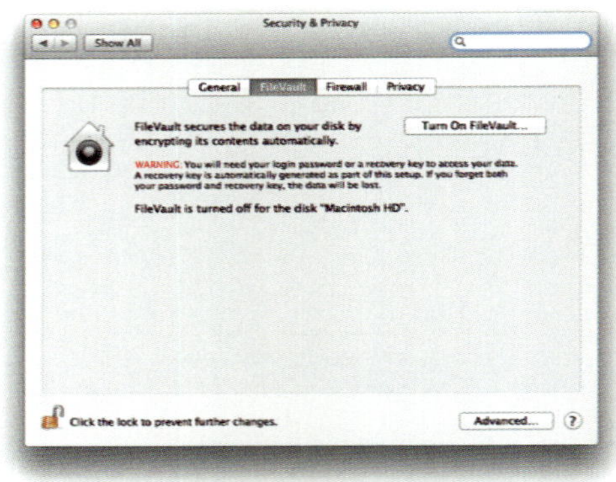

Figure 6-12 FileVault

3. Click the Turn on FileVault button.

Summary

In this chapter you have learnt how to set a password for your user account, how to enable the built-in firewall to help protect your MacBook, why it is important to run anti-virus software and how to keep your MacBook up to date.

7

The App Store

One of the great features of Mac OS X Mountain Lion is the App Store. The App Store provides both paid and free software that you can search for and download. The software includes games, music software, productivity tools and so much more. It also handles updates to the software and allows you to view reviews and even add your own review.

Launching the App Store

If you have the App Store installed, it will appear in the Dock, as shown in Figure 7-1.

Figure 7-1 The App Store in the Dock

1. Click on the App Store icon to open the App Store.

2. When the App Store opens, you will be presented with the Featured screen, as shown in Figure 7-2. This screen shows various items, including new and noteworthy apps.

Figure 7-2 Items in the App Store

Searching for and Selecting Apps

If you know what app you want, you can either search for it using the Search box, or you can click through various categories, as shown in Figure 7-3.

Figure 7-3 Categories in the App Store

So let's say that you want an app that you can use for Twitter. Perform the following steps to locate and download the app:

1. In the Search box, type in Twitter and press enter.
2. The results will be displayed for you, as shown in Figure 7-4. As you can see, some of the apps are shown as FREE, and some have a cost associated with them. The choice is yours, just click on the one you are interested in, or want to find out more about.

Figure 7-4 The Search Results

> There are often free and paid versions of the same software available. The free version might contain adverts and be limited in some way. If you are not sure about the app you want to buy, trying the free version first can be useful.

3. Information on that app will then be displayed, as shown in Figure 7-5. If you decide that it is the one you want, click on the Free button or Price button depending on what type of app it is.

Figure 7-5 Information on an app in the App Store

4. You will be asked to sign in using your Apple ID, as shown in Figure 7-6. Enter your details and click Sign In.

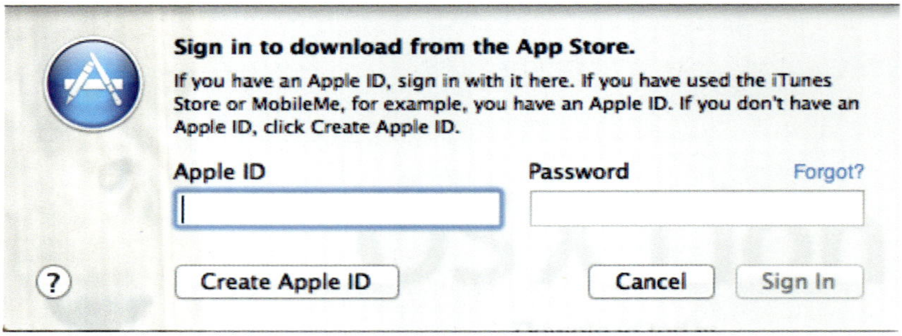

Figure 7-6 Sign in with your Apple ID

> If you don't yet have an Apple ID, click on the Create Apple ID button and work through the steps to create one. You will need a credit card to sign up, even if the app is free.

5. If this is the first time you have used the Apple ID on the Mac you may be asked to verify your account – do so if requested.

6. The app will now be downloaded and installed for you and you can then start using it straight away.

Your Purchase History

Every time you download something from the App Store, even if it is a free app, it is recorded in your Purchase History. This can be useful if you think you may have tried an app in the past and can't remember.

If you want to check your purchase history, just click Purchases from the App Store menu.

You will then be presented with a list of everything you have "purchased" and whether or not it is currently installed, as shown in Figure 7-7.

Figure 7-7 Your Purchase History

Updating App Store Purchases

As with the OS and its built-in software, apps in the App Store also need to be updated from time to time.

To check if there are any available updates, click on Updates from the App Store menu.

If there are any updates available they will be displayed and you can choose to update them, or if nothing needs updating you will be told 'No Updates Available', as shown in Figure 7-8.

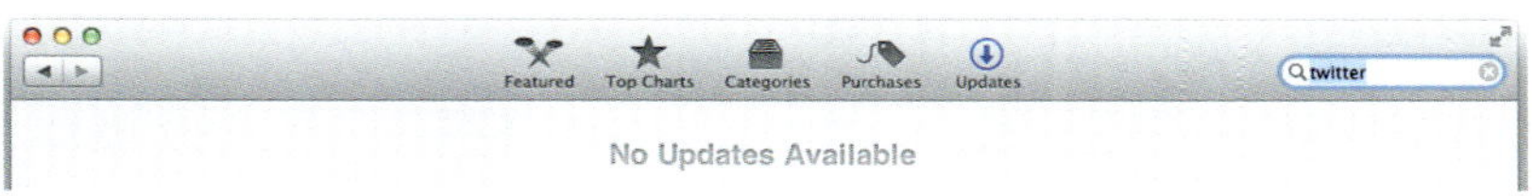

Figure 7-8

Removing an App

If you have tried an app and you no longer want it on your Mac, you will have to remove it. Unlike Windows, there isn't an Add/Remove Programs area that you can scroll through and choose to delete.

On the Mac, you just find the app using Finder and drag it to the Trash bin, which will remove the app for you.

> You have to use Finder to locate the app and drag it to the Trash bin otherwise it won't work. If you drag something from the Dock to the trash it only removes it from the Dock and you can't use the Applications folder from the Dock either – only through Finder will it be removed.

So to remove an app you no longer want, do the following:

> This procedure is the same for removing apps from the App Store or removing anything else that is installed on your Mac.

1. Ensure the app is closed and anything you might want to keep is saved.
2. Click on the Finder icon on the Dock.
3. Click on Applications from the FAVOURITES group, as shown in Figure 7-9, to display all the apps.

Figure 7-9 Installed Applications

4. Click and drag the app you want to remove to the Trash.
5. You will then be asked to type in your password to allow Finder to make the changes, as shown in Figure 7-10. Type it in and click OK.

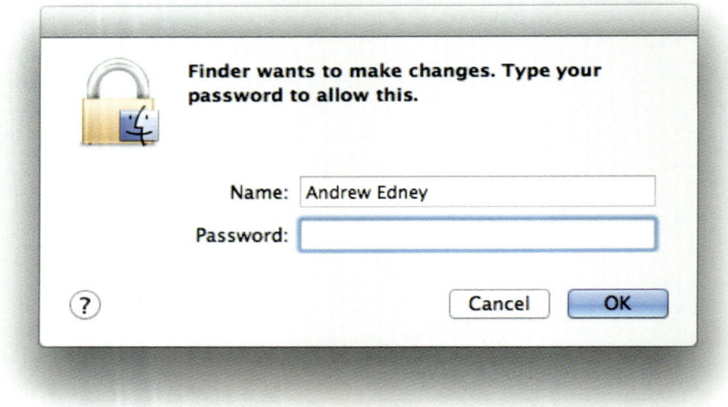

Figure 7-10 Allowing Finder to make changes

> Your App Store Purchase history will still show the app, even though you have removed it, but now will give you the option to install it again with a click, rather than you having to search for it again.

Summary

In this chapter you have learnt about the App Store and how to select and install apps. You have also learnt how easy it is to remove an app when you are finished with it. In the next chapter we will take a look at how you protect your data by backing up your Mac.

8

Backing Up Your Mac

Most people don't bother to back up their files – mainly because they don't think they will ever have a problem. Take it from me, it's not a case of if you will lose data, but when you will lose it! Therefore it is very important to back up your files, and do it regularly. But it's not just your files you want to back up – what about your programs and your settings?

Well Apple provide a program to do all of that. It's called Time Machine, and it's part of your Mac OS – all you have to do is configure it and let it do its own thing.

Time Machine keeps:

- Hourly backups for the past 24 hours
- Daily backups for the past month
- Weekly backups for all previous months

The oldest backups are deleted as and when the hard drive becomes full.

> Apple sells a device called Time Capsule, as shown in Figure 8-1. Time Capsule is a backup device that works wirelessly with Time Machine so you don't have to worry about remembering to connect a drive, it will backup automatically whenever you are connected to your home network.
>
> You can learn more from the Apple website here: http://www.apple.com/uk/timecapsule/

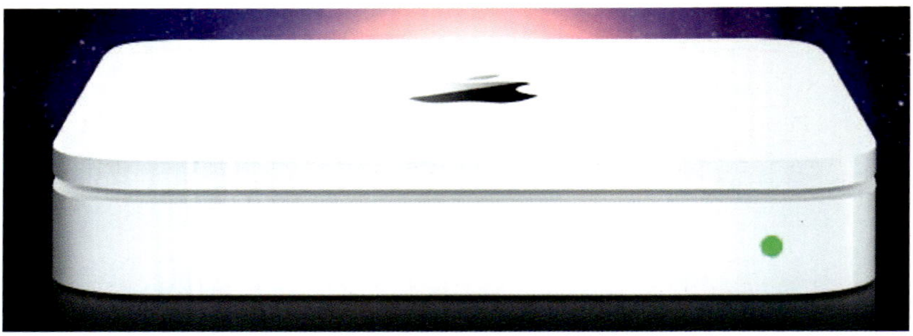

Figure 8-1 A Time Capsule device from Apple

Preparing a Hard Drive for Time Machine

The backups that Time Machine performs are written to an external USB hard drive. The idea behind this is to not only protect your data away from the Mac you are backing up (what would be the point of storing the backup on the Mac itself if your Mac got damaged or stolen?) but also so that you could store the drive "offsite".

> What I mean when I say "offsite" is that you can take that external USB hard drive with its Time Machine backups on and store it somewhere outside of your home – say at another family member's house. The idea being that you have a copy of your data away from your house in case of a disaster.

You will need an external USB hard drive that has enough space for the backups – I would recommend at least a 500GB hard drive, or more, depending on how much data you have and how frequently you want to backup your data.

> I would actually recommend that you get two USB drives. That way you can rotate them having one offsite and one onsite at all times.

You can purchase a hard drive that is Mac compatible or you can just get any hard drive and format it for use on the Mac.

If you have purchased a Mac compatible hard drive you should just be able to plug it in and skip to the next section.

If you have an old drive, or you are not sure if it is compatible or not, you will have to format it for use with the Mac.

To format the drive, perform the following steps:

> Formatting the hard drive will result in all the files on the drive being lost, so make sure you have copied or moved all the data from the drive you want to keep before continuing.

1. Plug the hard drive into a spare USB port on your Mac.
2. Click on the Launchpad icon on the Dock.
3. Find and click on the 'Other folder', as shown in Figure 8-2.

Figure 8-2 Open the Other folder

4. Click on 'Disk Utility' as shown in Figure 8-3.

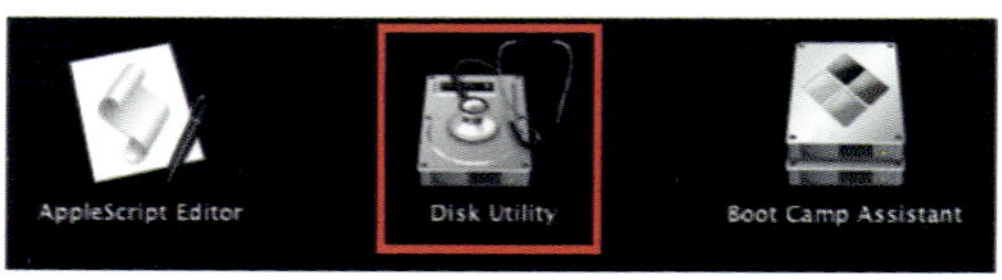

Figure 8-3 Selecting the Disk Utility application

5. Click on the USB hard drive in the left column, as shown in Figure 8-4.

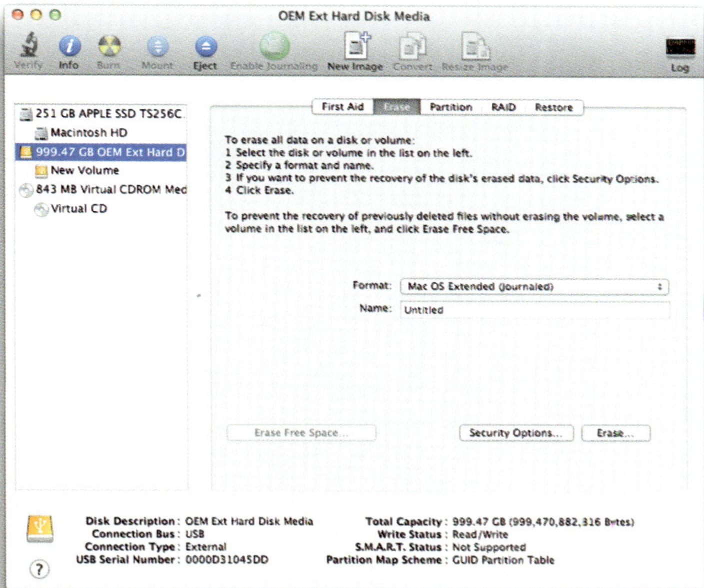

Figure 8-4 Erasing the drive

6. Click on the Erase button.
7. Select 'Mac OS Extended (Journaled)' from the drop-down list, as shown in Figure 8-5. Name the drive if you want to, then click on Erase.

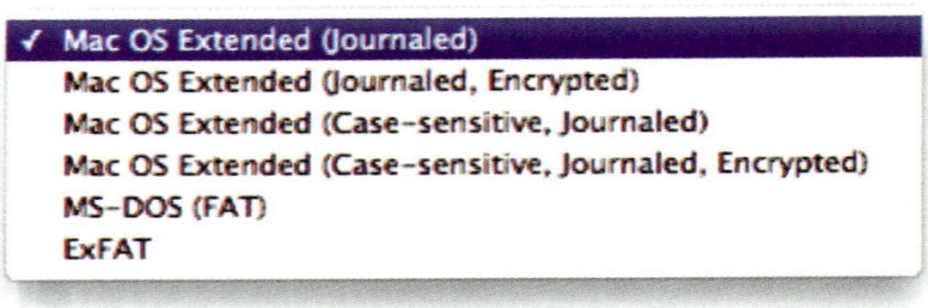

Figure 8-5 Choosing the drive format

8. Confirm you are sure you want to erase the disk, as shown in Figure 8-6 by clicking on the Erase button again.

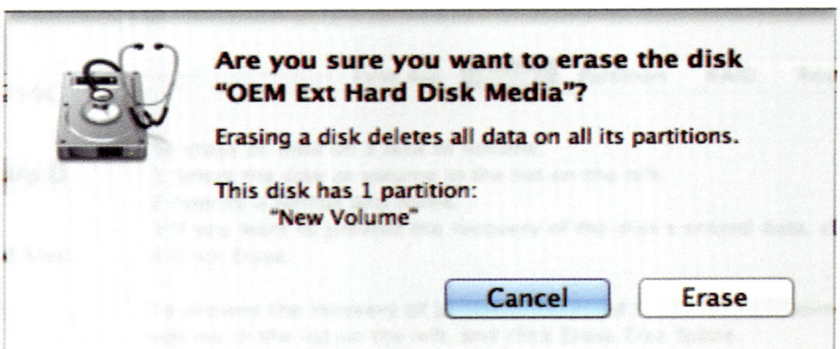

Figure 8-6 Making sure you really do want to erase the disk

9. You will now be presented with the option to use the drive with Time Machine, as shown in Figure 8-7. You

can either select 'Decide Later' or 'Use as Backup Disk'.

Figure 8-7 Do you want to use the drive with Time Machine?

Configuring and Using Time Machine

Now you have a usable hard drive, to use it with Time Machine and perform your first backup, do the following:

1. Ensure the drive is connected to your Mac
2. From the menu bar, click on the Time Machine logo, as shown in Figure 8-8.

Figure 8-8 Clicking on Time Machine

3. Click on 'Open Time Machine Preferences' from the drop-down menu, as shown in Figure 8-9.

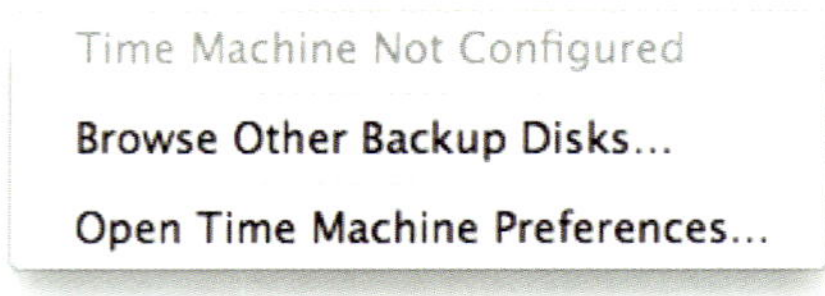

Figure 8-9 Selecting Time Machine Preferences

4. You will now see the Time Machine screen, as shown in Figure 8-10. Click on 'Select Backup Disk'.

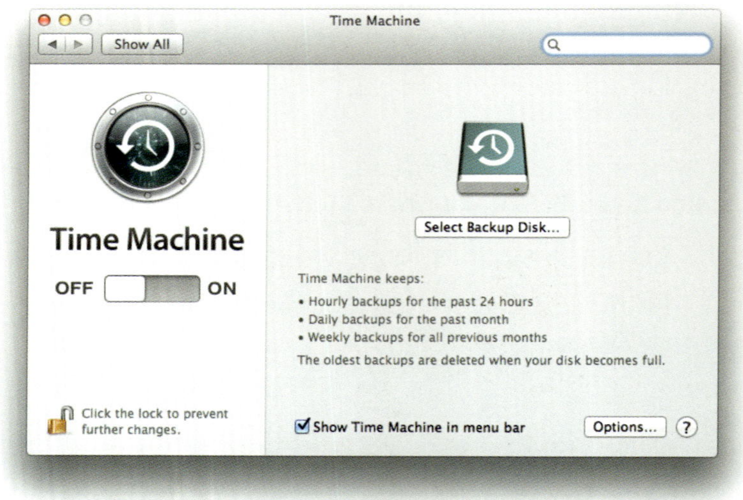

Figure 8-10 The Time Machine screen

5. Select your external hard drive from the list of available backup disks by clicking on it, as shown in Figure 8-11 and click 'Use Disk'.

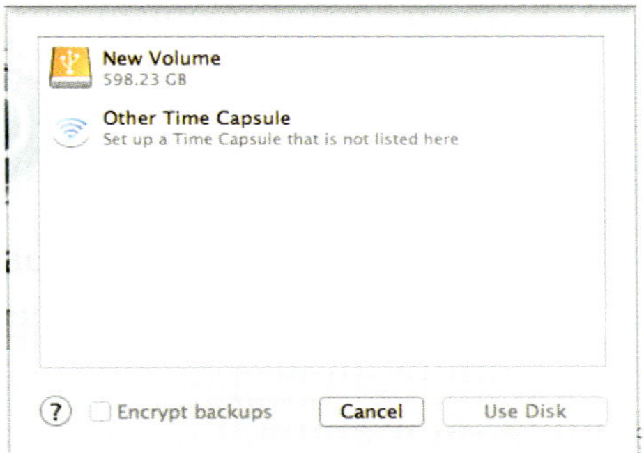

Figure 8-11 Selecting the drive to use

The backup will now be scheduled to start shortly, as shown in Figure 8-12.

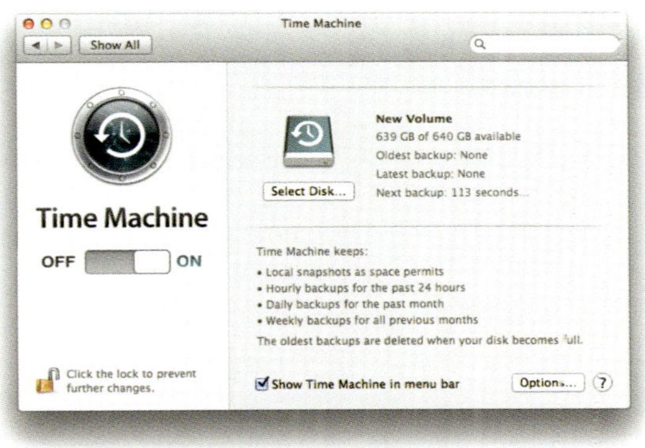

Figure 8-12 The backup will start shortly

You can now leave the drive connected while you are working to ensure that your Mac is backed up every hour.

> Remember to be patient with the backup process. This can take a while depending on how much data you actually have. And each time the backup should be quicker as it won't have to backup any files that haven't changed since the last backup.

If you want to disable Time Machine, you just have to click the switch to OFF. You can of course switch it back on at any time.

If you disable Time Machine, it disables the automatic backup. If you want to just perform a manual backup, do the following:

1. From the menu bar, click on the Time Machine icon.
2. Click on 'Back Up Now' from the drop-down list.

Time Machine Options

There are a few options that you can set for Time Machine if you want to.

These include the ability to exclude items from a backup and also to allow backups to take place while running on battery power (which is the default option). This of course will reduce your battery life so you may want to consider whether to keep that on. But to be honest, if you have the backup drive connected you probably want to perform a backup and are either connected to the power or are willing to accept the quicker battery drain in order to be protected.

To make changes to the Time Machine options, perform the following:

1. From the Time Machine screen, click on Options.
2. From the Options screen, shown in Figure 8-13, make whatever changes you want to make and then click Save. If you want to exclude something, click on the + sign and then choose whatever it is you want to exclude.

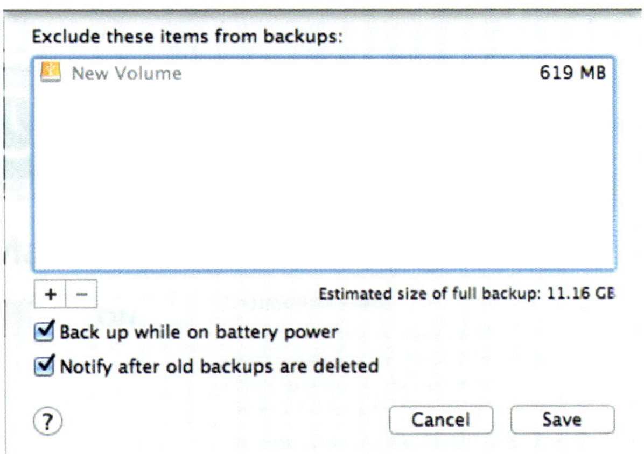

Figure 8-13 Excluding items from a Time Machine backup

Restoring Using Time Machine

Now that you have your files, settings and programs backed up using Time Machine, you should be protected in the event of a problem.

If you do have a problem, you can use Time Machine to recover a file, folders or even the entire Mac.

> If you want to recover your entire Mac, say for example because you have a new hard drive installed, you should run the Mac Recovery process (as described in the Mac documentation) and when you are given the option, choose to recover using Time Machine.

If you just want to recover a file or folders, you can do so with a few simple clicks, as follows:

1. Ensure the backup disk is connected to the Mac.
2. From the Dock, click on the Launchpad icon, and then on the Time Machine icon.
3. You can now scroll through all the backups (as shown in Figure 8-14) using the arrows on the right of the screen until you find the backup you want.
4. Find the file or files you want to recover and click on them.
5. Now click on Restore.

Figure 8-14 Selecting a specific Time Machine backup

The file or files will then be restored to their original location.

> You can choose to have the files restored to any location you wish – this can be very useful if you can't remember where they were originally or you just want them somewhere else.

Identifying Backup Disks

If you have multiple external hard drives, you might forget which drives are backup drives. Fortunately when you connect a drive to your Mac, if it has been configured as a backup drive, the icon displaying the drive on the desktop is different as it shows the Time Machine logo, shown in Figure 8-15.

Figure 8-15 Time Machine backup disk icon

As you can see from Figure 8-16, a non backup drive is displayed differently, showing a yellow drive with a USB logo.

Figure 8-16 USB disk icon

Summary

In this chapter you have learnt how to backup and restore files on your Mac using Time Machine and an external USB hard drive. I cannot stress enough the importance of backing up your files! In the next chapter we will take a look at things you can buy for your Mac to enhance your experience.

9

Applications on Your Mac

Earlier in the book we looked at how you can download free applications and buy applications from the Apple App Store. In this chapter we will take a look at some of the various applications that come as part of Mountain Lion.

Surfing the Internet with Safari

If you want to surf the Internet, then you will need a web browser. Apple provides a web browser called Safari.

Safari appears in the Dock, as shown in Figure 9-1.

Figure 9-1 Safari in the Dock

Safari looks and acts like any other web browser, as you can see in Figure 9-2.

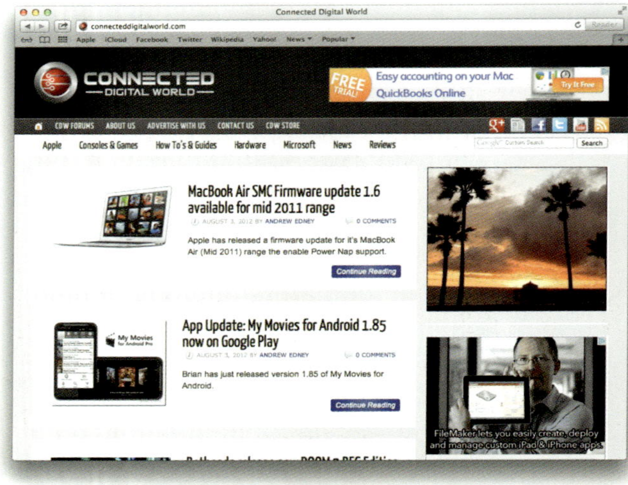

Figure 9-2 Surfing the Internet with Safari

One of the really nice things about Safari is that it provides a visual display of the sites you visit regularly. This display is called Top Sites, as shown in Figure 9-3, and it is automatically updated every time you use Safari. You can easily visit one of these sites by just clicking on the relevant window.

> If you don't want to use Safari you can always download and install any other supported web browser, such as Firefox.

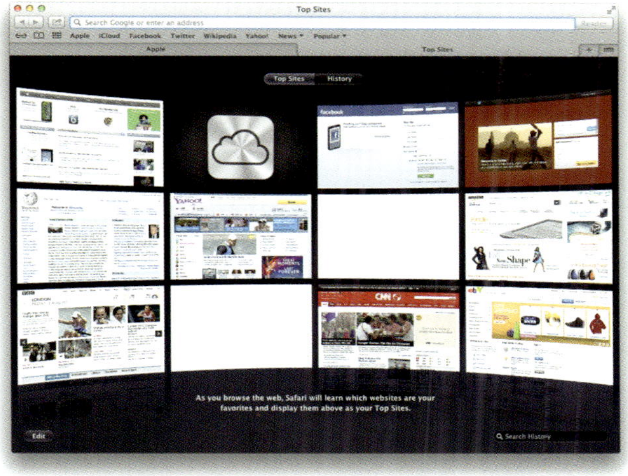

Figure 9-3 The Top Sites view in Safari

The Dashboard

The Dashboard is a collection of useful widgets that include anything from a calculator to a flight tracker. You can access them at any time and you can add your own as well.

To launch the Dashboard and select your widgets:

1. Click on the Mission Control icon in the Dock, as shown in Figure 9-4.

Figure 9-4 Mission Control on the Dock

2. Click on the Dashboard window.

This will display the default widgets, as shown in Figure 9-5.

Figure 9-5 Widgets on the Dashboard

3. To add a widget to the Dashboard, click on the + sign that will be displayed.
4. Scroll through the available widgets, as shown in Figure 9-6 and click on any that you want to add.

Figure 9-6 Adding new widgets

5. You can now drag the new widget, as shown in Figure 9-7 to any position on the desktop.

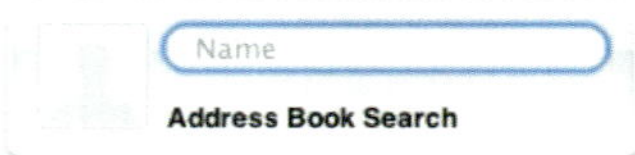

Figure 9-7 A new widget

6. If you click on the Widgets icon from the available widgets you can disable some of the widgets, as shown in Figure 9-8.

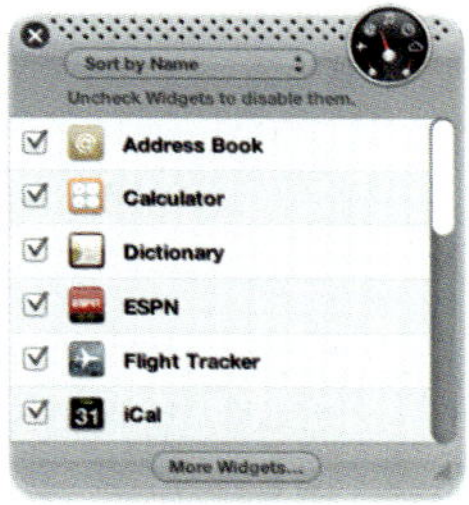

Figure 9-8 Disabling widgets

7. You can even download new widgets by clicking on the More Widgets button to connect to the Apple website which displays all available widgets. You are then able to select others, as shown in Figure 9-9.

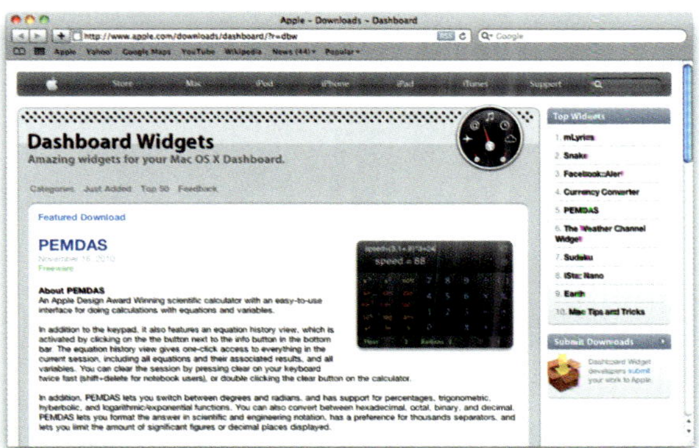

Figure 9-9 Downloading new widgets

iCal

iCal provides a useful calendar feature in order to keep track of your important appointments.

To use iCal:

1. Click on the iCal icon in the Dock, as shown in Figure 9-10.

Figure 9-10 iCal in the Dock

2. iCal will open and display the current day (along with whatever view is selected) as shown in Figure 9-11.

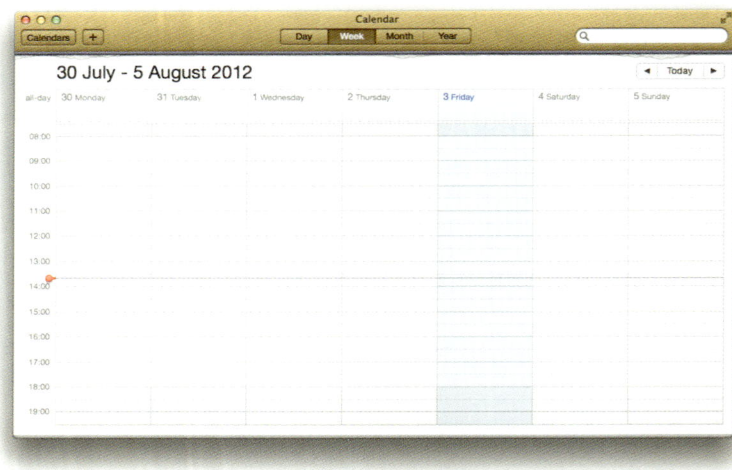

Figure 9-11 Your Calendar

3. To add something to the calendar just select the time-period and type in the appointment details.

Address Book

Address Book is exactly what is sounds like – it's an address book for keeping all your contact information in, including names, addresses, phone numbers and email details. You can even create your own groups so that you can split out work contacts from home contacts.

To start using Address Book:

1. Click on the Address Book icon from the Dock, as shown in Figure 9-12.

Figure 9-12 Address Book in the Dock

2. Your address book will then be displayed, as shown in Figure 9-13.
3. If you want to add something, click on the + icon in whichever column you wish to add an entry to.

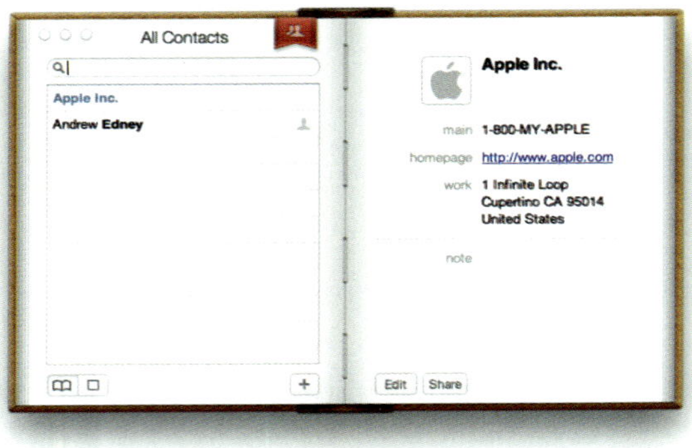

Figure 9-13 Your Address Book

4. Depending on what you want to add, you will need to complete as many of the details as you wish, as shown in Figure 9-14.

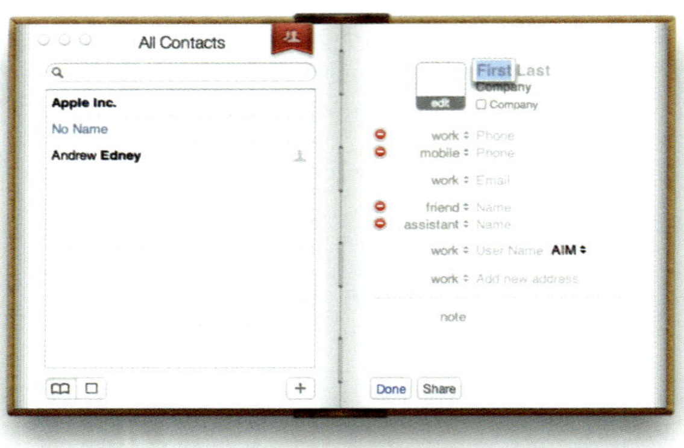

Figure 9-14 Entering a new contact

iLife '11

Apple have a suite of applications they call iLife, and the latest iteration of this suite is iLife '11, as shown in Figure 9-15. If you have purchased a Mac recently you should have iLife '11 pre-installed.

Figure 9-15 iLife '11

> If you don't have iLife '11 pre-installed, or you have an older version of iLife then you can upgrade from the Apple Store or buy the apps individually from the App Store.

iLife '11 contains three different applications. They are iPhoto, which enables you to browse, edit and share you photos, as shown in Figure 9-16.

Figure 9-16 iPhoto

iPhoto is a really good application, and it even automatically imports your pictures directly from your camera when you connect it up. These makes it very easy to use straight away. iPhoto also enables you to access your photos based on various criteria, including by location – so if you wanted to view all your holiday pictures you can easily.

There is also iMovie, which enables you to create your own movies, add titles and effects, and a whole lot more, as shown in Figure 9-17.

iMovie provides everything you would expect from an expensive video editing package and it is very easy to use.

You can even import photos from iPhoto and use them within your video production exploits. Why not put together a video of your holiday and show all your friends and family?

Figure 9-17 iMovie

And last, but not least is GarageBand, which provides everything you need to create your own songs and music.

> If you want to learn more about the features of iLife '11, take a look at the Apple website:
>
> http://www.apple.com/uk/ilife

Other Applications

There are a number of other applications that come as part of Mountain Lion that are not shown on the Dock.

Launchpad, as shown in Figure 9-18, is a capability that displays your available applications in the same way that you would view them on an iPad.

Figure 9-18 Launchpad

If you click on the Launchpad icon on the Dock you will see what is available, as shown in Figure 9-19.

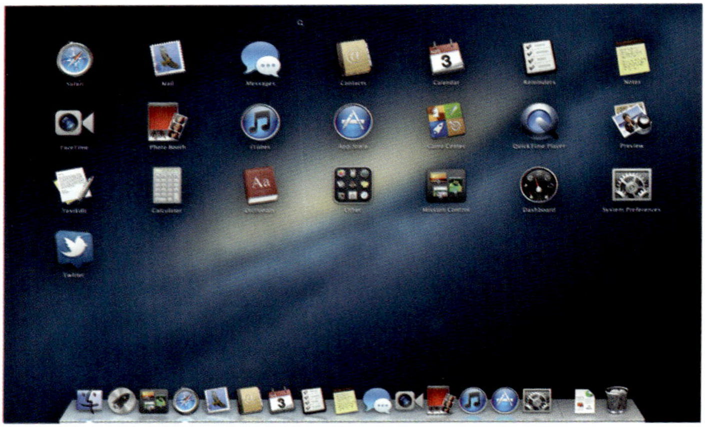

Figure 9-19 Available applications

Any applications that you download and install will also appear here.

Messages

Messages is an application that enables you to send instant messages to other Mountain Lion users, and also to users running other iOS devices, such as an iPhone or iPad who have the iMessage capability.

To use Messages you need to initially configure it.

1. To configure Messages, click on the Messages icon in the dock, as shown in Figure 9-20.

Figure 9-20 Selecting Messages from the Dock

2. You then need to sign in with your Apple ID (if you are not already signed in).
3. You will then see the Messages application as shown in Figure 9-21.

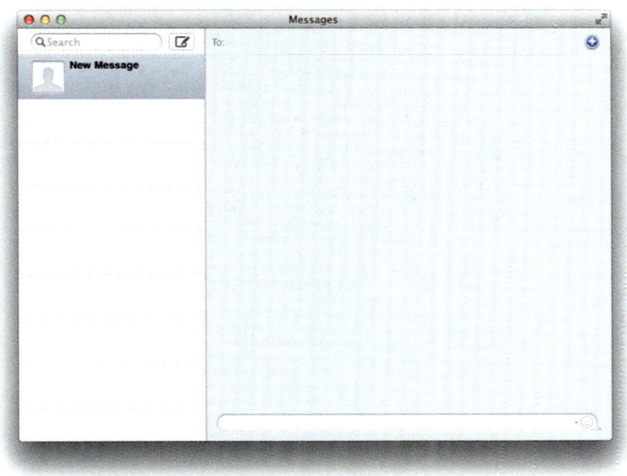

Figure 9-21 Messages

4. You can then click on New Message and select a contact from your address book to start an iMessage conversation with.
5. You can also just type the email address of the person you want to message (as long as they have their email address associated with iMessage).
6. Then just start typing away.

You need to be connected to a network or the Internet for Messages to work.

7. When you have finished your discussion you can just close down Messages.

Summary

In this chapter you have learnt about some of the built-in applications that come with Mountain Lion. There is plenty of software available for the Mac so why not have a look today to see if there is anything else you need and give it a try?

10

Troubleshooting

I would love to tell you that nothing will ever go wrong with your Mac, but then I would be lying. Things do go wrong. It could be a corrupt file, a problem with an application, a disk failure. Whatever it is, when something does go wrong you will need to troubleshoot it and try to resolve it. I could write an entire book on troubleshooting and it would still not cover every possible problem and issue. Instead, in this short chapter I will just cover a few items.

> Whatever the issue – DON'T PANIC! Now we have that out of the way, the best thing to do is to check online for a solution to your problem if you can't figure it out yourself or any steps you do take don't end up working. Remember there is a pretty good help system built-in to Mountain Lion, so why not give that a try?

Forcing an Application to Quit

Sometimes an application just won't shut down. It does happen from time to time. If it does happen to you, you can force that application to quit:

1. Click on the Apple logo in the menu bar.
2. From the drop-down list, click on Force Quit.
3. Select the application from the displayed list, as shown in Figure 10-1, and click on Force Quit.

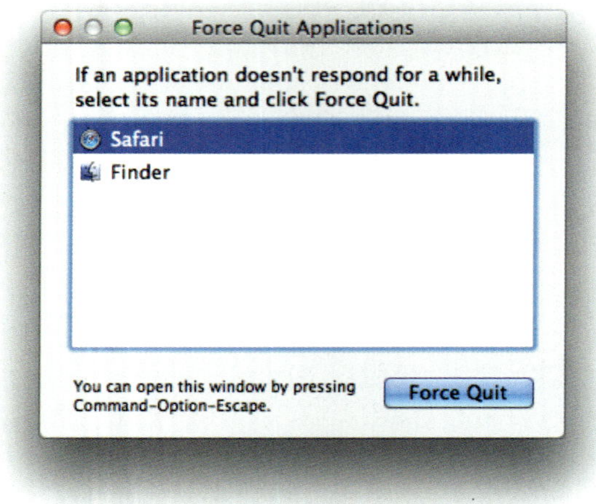

Figure 10-1 Force Quit an application

Safe Boot and Safe Mode

Sometimes when you try to boot up your Mac something goes wrong and it just won't boot correctly. Maybe you installed something that is causing a conflict? You can start your Mac using Safe Boot. What Safe Boot does is start your Mac in a special way, checking various files and disabling any Non Apple start-up items, thus allowing you to boot into Safe Mode and hopefully fix the issue. This is exactly the same as Safe Mode in Windows.

To activate Safe Boot and start in Safe Mode:

1. When the Mac is switched off, press the power button to start up the Mac as usual only this time hold down the SHIFT key during boot.
2. When the boot process has completed, you will be asked to enter your password to log in, as shown in Figure 10-2. Just enter your password as usual and click on the Log In button.
3. Try to resolve the problem (I know that sounds a little vague but each problem will be different). If, for example, you have just installed a new piece of software and you are fairly sure that this has caused the problem you should uninstall it (remember we showed you how to do that earlier in the book) and try rebooting your Mac. If that resolves the problem then you should investigate a possible solution if you want to use that piece of software. If it doesn't solve it then you keep looking, and remember that the Internet is

your friend when it comes to finding possible solutions.

Figure 10-2 Safe Boot into the Mac

Giving Up and Starting Again

Sometimes you may have no choice but to just give up and start again. OK, that might sound a little extreme, but if you have a major hardware failure, say for example your hard drive fails or is experiencing major problems it would be a wise idea to just perform a clean install (or recovery) of the Mac OS.

Depending on which Mac you have, the reinstall / recovery process might be a little different so take a look at the manual that came with your Mac for more information on just how to do this.

Don't forget that if you have a Time Machine backup you could either try recovering some of the files from there or when you perform the reinstallation you can select a Time Machine backup to recover as part of the process, thus returning your Mac to the state that it was in before the problems occurred. This works very well and has saved me on more than one occasion – so make sure you perform Time Machine backups regularly as you never know when you might need them.

Summary

In this chapter you have learnt a few tips for troubleshooting some problems that might occur on your Mac. So if you take nothing else away from this chapter, remember this – searching for your specific problem on the Internet can often help find a quick solution. If you are really not sure what to do, you could always contact Apple if your Mac is still within support or visit an Apple Store if you have one near to you.

Index

Also Available by the Same Author

- £7.99
- ISBN 978 0 85934 733 4